RADICAL RULERS

THE WHITE HOUSE ELITES WHO ARE PUSHING AMERICA TOWARD SOCIALISM

ROBERT KNIGHT

TRUTH IN *Action* MINISTRIES™

Formerly
CORAL RIDGE MINISTRIES

Fort Lauderdale, Florida

RADICAL RULERS

*This book is dedicated
to my wife Barbara*

CONTENTS

TOO "THRILLED" TO REPORT THE RADICAL TRUTH

"We're just five days away from fundamentally transforming the United States of America."[1]

—Barack Hussein Obama, October 31, 2008

This book is about the "radical rulers" that have come to power in Washington and what they are trying to accomplish. It's about what political analyst and former Clinton Administration insider Dick Morris calls "a bloodless coup."

Barack Hussein Obama was elected in 2008 as a "unifier," a reasonable guy who could help America get beyond its racial problems. His rhetorical gifts are undeniable. Overall, he conveys the aura of a skilled "bargainer," as Hoover Institution scholar and author Shelby Steele wrote before the election.

The media aggressively airbrushed out Obama's radical background and questionable associations. At every step in the process, Mr. Obama enjoyed overwhelmingly favorable press and benefited from volleys of attacks on anyone standing in his way. Once they had made up their minds that Obama was the One, for instance, the media threw Hillary Clinton overboard, treating her like ... a Republican. After years of positive press, it's understandable that she found it difficult to hide her anger and surprise.

FREE RIDE

Even in the presidential primary debates, Obama got a free ride, so much so that the liberal writers of NBC's *Saturday Night Live* presented skits in which journalists rudely pummeled an actress playing Hillary Clinton while bowing and scraping to the actor portraying Mr. Obama. Later, *SNL* used comedienne Tina Fey's dead-on impression of GOP Vice Presidential nominee Sarah Palin to caricature her as a ditz. The news networks compliantly aired lots of clips of Fey, thus confusing the public about what Palin had actually said.

In October 2008, during an exchange in Toledo, Ohio, Joe "the Plumber" Wurzelbacher elicited Obama's comment, "I think when you spread the wealth around, it's good for everybody."[2] That gave the nation a glimpse into Obama's redistributionist mindset. But instead of examining more of Obama's background and views, the press went after ... Joe the Plumber.[3]

Although some of Obama's extraordinary and disturbing background leaked out during the campaign, the press largely covered it up. Acting more like smitten lovers than skeptical journalists, they heaped praise upon him daily, while sniping at his opponent, John McCain, and especially his running mate, Mrs. Palin.

A study by the Media Research Center's (MRC) Culture and Media Institute, for example, revealed that out of 69 network segments on Sarah Palin in a two-week period surrounding the vice presidential debate, 37 were negative and only two were positive. The rest were neutral.[4] In sharp contrast, Obama and his running mate Joe Biden got what amounted to a press agent's dream: upbeat, relentlessly positive reports bordering on the sycophantic. During the primary campaign, for example, the Big Three networks carried 463 positive stories on Obama compared to 70 with negative content, according to another MRC study.[5]

Some journalists sheepishly admitted after the election that the press had gone way over the line. Others continued the sycophancy. *Newsweek*'s Evan Thomas, grandson of Socialist Party presidential candidate Norman Thomas, gushed on MSNBC's *Hardball* after Obama's June 5, 2009, speech in Cairo:

> I mean, in a way Obama's standing above the country, above — above the world; he's sort of God.[6]

Thomas went on to demean Ronald Reagan for being "parochial," and "all about America." By contrast, Obama is: "'we are above that now.'"

He wasn't about to get an argument from host Chris Matthews, who famously blurted out on primary election night:

> It's part of reporting this case, this election, the feeling most people get when they hear Barack Obama's speech. My, I felt this thrill going up my leg. I mean, I don't have that too often.[7]

In similar fashion, the press overwhelmingly favored liberal candidates for Congress. Many people were fed up with a Republican leadership that had created new entitlement programs, increased federal spending and had become in some ways indistinguishable from their liberal Democrat colleagues across the aisle. The Democrats took control of Congress in 2006, but it was not until 2009, when they controlled both houses of Congress and the White House, that the truly radical surge in government growth began in earnest.

HOSTILE TAKEOVER

To some Americans, particularly those who don't live in the liberal Northeast or on the Left Coast, it feels like America was conquered by hostile, alien invaders who are determined to wipe out the most Christian, liberty-loving nation in the history of the world and replace it with a top-down, government-run secular socialist kleptocracy similar to some of the corrupt regimes in Europe. "Hope and change" has morphed quickly into "do it or else."

A cursory look at some of the congressional leadership speaks volumes. The Speaker of the House is Nancy Pelosi, who represents an ultra-Left district in San Francisco that is home to an annual homosexual sado-masochistic street fair.[8] Pelosi is an advocate for the entire left-wing agenda, from abortion on demand, to gay activism, to exponential government growth and financial profligacy.

The Chairman of the House Banking Committee is none other than Rep. Barney Frank, the openly homosexual Massachusetts congressman with a 100 percent rating from NARAL Pro Choice America and other leftist groups. *The Wall Street Journal* says Frank was one of the most aggressive advocates for government threats against banks to violate their lending standards and issue loans to people who could not afford to pay them back.[9] The resulting subprime mortgage market crash played a major role in the onset of the 2008-2009 recession.

In 2004, Rep. Frank and several other Democrats testified at a hearing that the federal housing giants Fannie Mae and Freddie Mac were just fine and suggested that Bush Administration efforts to inquire into possible abuses and dangers of the agencies' promotion of unsecured (except by taxpayers) subprime mortgages smacked of racism.[10] Incredibly, this man is still making financial policy for the nation in his powerful post. His colleague, Rep. Maxine Waters (D) of Los Angeles, stated flatly at the same hearing, "We do not have a crisis at Freddie Mac, and particularly at Fannie Mae."[11]

Back in California, Rep. Henry Waxman, who is the co-author of the cap and trade bill known as Waxman-Markey and which would strangle the U.S. economy with a massive, government-administered carbon credit system and astronomical energy taxes, hails from West Hollywood. Perhaps the most ultra-Left district south of San Francisco, West Hollywood is known for its Sybaritic lifestyles and radical politics. In 2004, Waxman even issued a profoundly misleading report[12] blasting abstinence education and promoting the condom-based approach that has led to millions of cases of sexually transmitted diseases.

Just to the east is Las Vegas, Nevada, represented by Senate Majority Leader Harry Reid, author of the 2,700-plus page government health care takeover bill and issuer of bald-faced threats and bribes with taxpayer money to buy votes. Finally, there's Assistant Majority Leader Dick Durbin, from Obama's Chicago, who once compared the actions of our troops at the Guantanamo Bay Detention Center to those of "Nazis, Soviets in their gulags or some mad regime — Pol Pot or others — that had no concern for human beings."[13]

Think about this for a moment. These people, along with Obama, are running our government. In effect, we have a radical axis from the two coasts, plus Chicago and Vegas, spending us into bankruptcy and creating a socialist state. There are many more culpable congressional leftists we could cite, but this radical Congress deserves its own book. *Radical Rulers* is about Mr. Obama and the people with whom he has populated his administration.

RADICAL CLIQUE OF MARXISTS

The election coverage and continuing press adulation of Obama goes beyond dereliction of duty and qualifies as a shocking scandal. But not just any scandal. Most political skullduggery involves the misuse of money. If only it were that simple. But this is about a "mainstream" media delivering an unsuspecting America into the hands of a radical clique of Marxists and other left-wing extremists who are determined to destroy the nation's moral foundations and free market system and replace it with European-style "green" socialism. There's also plenty of old-fashioned graft that has been covered up, especially in Obama's Chicago, but that is the least of it.

Veteran political analyst Victor Davis Hanson summarizes the Obama worldview and why it poses a threat to the idea of limited government:

> Obama combines the age-old belief that the state is there to level the playing field (rather than protect the rights of the individual and secure the safety of the people from foreign threats), with the postmodern notion that government must recompense those by fiat on the basis of their race or class or gender.[14]

In his first year in office, President Obama has "thrilled" the media by expanding government, promoting abortion and homosexuality, tripling the national debt, unveiling massive schemes to take over much of the economy, and assembling a team of "czars" and other appointees who are on the far left of the political spectrum. If every radical appointee were scrutinized, this would be a very long book. So we're going to take a look at a dozen or so people whose appointments shine a light into Obama's ideology and policy ambitions for the country.

Many of these first came to light on the Fox News Channel's *Glenn Beck Show* or on such websites as Breitbart.com, Accuracy in Media or from obscure bloggers who did a public service by doing the investigative reporting that the mainstream media refuse to do. "Green jobs czar" Van Jones, for instance, was outed as a self-avowed Communist by Trevor Loudon, a blogger from New Zealand.[15] What's more, Jones was revealed to be a "truther," that is, one of the crackpots who believe that the Bush Administration was behind the 9/11 terrorist attacks. Neither the *New York Times,* the *Washington Post* nor the major news networks other than Fox ran stories about the Jones allegations until he had issued two apologies shortly before resigning.

The media, even when embarrassed by a constant flow of revelations that they themselves should have covered, are sticking to their excuse: They blame the White House "vetting process," as if the radical records now surfacing are a complete surprise.

But Thomas Sowell curtly dismisses that argument:

> Those who say that the Obama administration should have investigated those people more thoroughly before appointing them are missing the point completely. Why should we assume that Barack Obama didn't know what such people were like, when he has been associating with precisely these kinds of people for decades before he reached the White House?...
>
> Had it not been for the Fox News Channel, these stealth appointees might have remained unexposed for what they are. Fox News is now high on the administration's enemies list.[16]

Indeed, at least two Obama Administration officials declared that Fox is "not a legitimate news organization." White House communications director Anita Dunn, who resigned on November 9, 2009, said of Fox News, "It's opinion journalism masquerading as news"[17] and, "We're going to treat them the way we would treat an opponent."[18] She shocked a June high school commencement audience by quoting Red Chinese dictator Mao Tse Tung: Here's part of a clip of Dunn that Fox News Channel host Glenn Beck ran:

> .... the third lesson and tip actually comes from **two of my favorite political philosophers — Mao Tse Tung and Mother Teresa**, not often coupled with each other but **the two people that I turn to most to basically deliver a simple point**, which is you're going to make choices.
>
> .... In 1947, when Mao Tse Tung was being challenged

within his own party on his plan to basically take China over, Chiang Kai-Shek and the nationalist Chinese held the cities, they had the army. They had the air force. They had everything on their side, and people said how can you win? ... and Mao Tse Tung said, you know, "you fight your war, and I'll fight mine."[19]

She did not bother noting that under Mao, the Chinese Communists killed an estimated 60 million to 100 million people and created a slave state that Adolf Hitler would have envied. Without context, the students were left with an apparent endorsement of Mao.

Dunn dismissed criticism of her heavy-handed approach to Fox News in an interview with CNN, where she repeated her claim that Fox is not a "legitimate" news network, unlike, she said — CNN.[20]

This is, of course, just the tip of the iceberg. Before delving into a more detailed look at a few of the Obama Administration's appointees, it would help to look at the Man himself. A brief review paints a picture of a politician who is not appointing radical leftists as one more special interest group but as — comrades.

PART 1

BARACK OBAMA: RADICAL-IN-CHIEF

CHAPTER 1

RADICAL ROOTS

Even before Barack Obama was nominated, disturbing reports surfaced about his background and the people who helped him form his worldview. In large part, the mainstream media ignored it all, and even ridiculed anyone who dared to look into it.[21]

Names like radical pastor Jeremiah Wright and unrepentant Weather Underground terrorist William Ayers floated up now and then but were quickly pushed back down, much the way the media buried the Bill Clinton/Gennifer Flowers "bimbo eruptions" scandal during the 1992 primaries.

In 19 Democratic primary debates in 2007 and 2008, for example, Obama faced more "softball" questions than any other candidate. He was not asked any questions about his relationships with two of his more controversial associates — Jeremiah Wright and Nation of Islam leader Louis Farrakhan — until NBC's Tim Russert finally inquired on Feb. 28, 2008.[22]

He was not asked about his relationship with Ayers until the end.[23] On April 16, 2008, during the final Philadelphia Democratic primary debate,

ABC's George Stephanopoulos finally asked Obama:

> ...a gentleman named William Ayers. He was part of the Weather Underground in the 1970s. They bombed the Pentagon, the Capitol and other buildings. He's never apologized for that. And in fact, on 9/11 he was quoted in the *New York Times* saying, "I don't regret setting bombs; I feel we didn't do enough." An early organizing meeting for your state senate campaign was held at his house, and your campaign has said you are friendly. Can you explain that relationship for the voters, and explain to Democrats why it won't be a problem?

Here is Obama's response:

> George, but this is an example of what I'm talking about. This is a guy who lives in my neighborhood, who's a professor of English in Chicago, who I know and who I have not received some official endorsement from. He's not somebody who I exchange ideas from on a regular basis.
>
> And the notion that somehow as a consequence of me knowing somebody who engaged in detestable acts 40 years ago, when I was 8 years old, somehow reflects on me and my values, doesn't make much sense, George.

Ayers and his wife, fellow Weather Underground terrorist Bernardine Dorhn, had introduced Obama to Chicago politics with a party at their home when Obama was running for the state Senate. On March 2, 2001, Ayers contributed $200 to Obama's campaign.[24]

LINK TO BILL AYERS

Obama utterly misrepresented his relationship with Ayers, taking the dodge that he was only a child when Ayers orchestrated the bombings. What Obama left unsaid was Ayers' relationship with him — when both were adults

— on two boards: the Woods Fund, which Obama chaired from 1993 to 2001,[25] and which Ayers was a director for three of those years, and the Chicago Annenberg Challenge. Both organizations channeled grant money to mostly liberal/ left causes, including to Jeremiah Wright's Trinity United Church of Christ, and the Association of Community Organizations for Reform Now (ACORN).

Ayers today is an unreconstructed communist who is an education professor at the University of Illinois in Chicago. He wrote a glowing

President Barack Obama
Zuma/Michael Reynolds

endorsement for the back cover of the book *Queering Elementary Education*, a collection of essays about how to overcome "heterosexism" in schools and to institute pro-homosexual policies. Ayers has also promoted the homosexual agenda in schools in other ways.

Education writer and Mission America President Linda Harvey notes in her WorldNetDaily.com article, "Bill Ayers' gay agenda for your kids," that:

> In 2007, a group from the American Educational Research Association, or AERA, including Ayers, demanded [the] major accrediting organization for schools, colleges, and departments of education include categories of "social justice, sexual orientation and gender identity" in its standards. Ayers and colleagues called their effort "Call to Action: A RED Campaign for Social Justice and Queer Lives." Ayers, formerly vice president for curriculum of the AERA,

was the spokesman on behalf of the effort, calling on the National Council for Accreditation of Teacher Education, or NCATE, to include these categories.

What would an Obama administration do? The record shows that Obama supported Illinois Senate Bill 99 in 2003, which, despite denials by Obama and false claims by the mainstream media, was not a bill to protect children from sexual predators. It was a sweeping, comprehensive sex-education bill that lowered the age of instruction from sixth grade to kindergarten, gutted an abstinence emphasis and prohibited "bias" based on "sexual orientation."[26]

For more on Obama's homosexual agenda for school kids, see chapter eight on "safe schools czar" Kevin Jennings.

Ayers' wife Bernardine Dohrn, who was jailed for seven months for refusing to cooperate with a grand jury investigating the Weather Underground's murder of a security guard and two police officers in a Brinks truck robbery in 1981, is a clinical associate professor of law at Northwestern Law and the director of the Children and Family Law Center.[27] Apart from what this says about Obama's circle of friends, it also reveals the extent to which much of academia has fallen into the grip of the hard Left, where nothing — not even terrorism — is an employment disqualifier if you have "progressive" views.

The same goes for the media. Here's an excerpt from a report on FactCheck.org, in which the Annenberg Public Policy Center tried to deflect campaign ads by John McCain that had pointed to Obama's radical connections:

> Even the description of Ayers as a "terrorist" is a matter of interpretation. Setting off bombs can fairly be described as terrorism even when they are intended to cause only property damage, which is what Ayers has admitted doing in his youth. But for nearly three decades since, Ayers has lived the relatively quiet life of an educator. It would be correct to call him a "former terrorist," and an "unapologetic" one at that.[28]

Locally, Ayers' radical past hasn't been much of an

issue. *Chicago Sun-Times* columnist Lynn Sweet wrote last spring that it "was no big deal, or any deal, to any local political reporters or to the editorial boards of the *Sun-Times* or [Chicago] *Tribune*."[29]

Of course it was no big deal. The nation's newsrooms are dominated by the hard Left, which is why Americans are turning more and more to alternative media and why the Left is frantically trying to figure out ways to shut down conservative talk radio and even conservative Internet sites (see chapter seven on FCC "diversity czar" Mark Lloyd).

CONNECTION TO ACORN

As for ACORN, Obama served as a trainer, attorney, and organizer during his years in Chicago before running for office.

"Chicago is home to one of its strongest chapters, and Acorn has burst into a closed city council meeting there. Acorn protestors in Baltimore disrupted a bankers' dinner and sent four busloads of profanity-screaming protestors against the mayor's home, terrifying his wife and kids," writes *National Review*'s investigative writer Stanley Kurtz. In a May 2008 article, Kurtz warned about the Obama/ACORN connection, noting that the press had taken little interest:

> Obama's ties to Acorn — arguably the most politically radical large-scale activist group in the country — are wide, deep, and longstanding. If Acorn is adept at creating a non-partisan, inside-game veneer for what is, in fact an intensely radical, leftist, and politically partisan reality, so is Obama himself. This is hardly a coincidence: Obama helped train Acorn's leaders in how to play this game. For the most part, Obama seems to have favored the political-insider strategy, yet it's clear that he knew how to play the in-your-face "direct action" game as well. And surely during his many years of close association with Acorn, Obama had to know what the group was all about.... In any case,

if you're looking for the piece of the puzzle that confirms and explains Obama's network of radical ties, gather your Acorns this spring. Or next winter, you may just be left watching the "President from Acorn" at his feast.[30]

A BRIEF BIO

Born in 1961 in Honolulu, Hawaii, according to his official biography, Obama's radical connections stretch back to his own boyhood.

The White House website proclaims that:

His story is the American story – values from the heartland, a middle-class upbringing in a strong family....[31]

But Obama's family life was anything but typical or "strong." Raised largely by his American mother, Stanley Ann Dunham, and his maternal grandparents, he was abandoned by both his Kenyan birth father, Barack Hussein Obama Sr., a Muslim, and his stepfather Lolo Soetoro, also a nominal Muslim. Barack Obama was infused with an odd mixture of secular humanism from his non-believing mother and a smorgasbord of religious concepts he picked up along the way. His mother moved him and his half-sister, Maya Soetoro, from place to place.

From 1967 to 1971, in Indonesia, he attended a public Muslim school and then a Catholic school, where he was registered as a Muslim named Barry Soetoro, according to school records released on January 24, 2007, by the Fransiskus Assisi school in Jakarta.[32]

Obama eventually enrolled at Occidental College in Los Angeles. Although Snopes.com, the Web site that investigates myths, insists that Obama was not registered as a foreign student when he attended Occidental in 1979 and 1980, the website acknowledges that Obama's Occidental records remain sealed.[33]

Obama went on to graduate from Columbia University with a B.A. in international relations in 1983, and then went to Chicago, where he was a community organizer from 1985 to 1988 before attending Harvard Law School, where he received his law degree in 1991. He returned to Chicago, working for some law firms and, in 1992, for Project Vote, which is now an ACORN offshoot, registering voters. He was a constitutional law professor at the University of Chicago Law School from 1992 to 2004, during which time he ran for and won a state Senate seat and served three terms before being elected to the U.S. Senate in 2004, and then President in 2008.[34] Along the way, he did legal work for ACORN.

A number of lawsuits claim that Obama was born in Kenya, not Hawaii, and that an actual birth certificate from Hawaii indicating the hospital, doctor, and other information has never been released. This controversy, which the media have never fully vetted, is outside the scope of this book, however, which focuses on Obama's radical views and associates.

THE HAWAII YEARS

From 1971 to 1979, Obama spent his boyhood years with his maternal grandparents Madelyn and Stanley Armour Dunham in Hawaii, where he attended the exclusive college prep Punahou School.[35]

In his autobiography, *Dreams from My Father* (1995), Obama talked about evenings spent with "a poet named Frank."

The man in question is Frank Marshall Davis, who befriended the young Obama in Hawaii, where Davis was a columnist for the Communist Party newspaper, the *Honolulu Record*.

New Zealand blogger Trevor Loudon, who later broke the story of Obama "green jobs czar" appointee Van Jones' communism, first reported[36] in 2007 that the mysterious "Frank" was in fact, the communist Mr. Davis, a fact later confirmed by a Davis biographer at the University of Hawaii. Loudon had discovered an online article in the Communist Party journal *Political Affairs* by contributing editor Gerald Horne, a history professor at the University of Houston, who had written that Davis:

> "befriended" a "Euro-American family" that had "migrated to Honolulu from Kansas and a young woman from this family eventually had a child with a young student from Kenya East Africa who goes by the name of Barack Obama, who retracing the steps of Davis eventually

decamped to Chicago."[37]

Cliff Kincaid, of Accuracy in Media and USASurvival.org, summarizes research from veteran anti-communist researcher Herb Romerstein's paper, "Communism in Hawaii and the Obama Connection."[38]

> The record shows that Obama was in Hawaii from 1971-1979, where, at some point in time, he developed a close relationship, almost like a son, with Davis, listening to his "poetry" and getting advice on his career path. But Obama, in his book, *Dreams from My Father,* refers to him repeatedly as just "Frank."[39]
>
> The reason is apparent: Davis was a known communist who belonged to a party subservient to the Soviet Union. In fact, the 1951 report of the Commission on Subversive Activities to the Legislature of the Territory of Hawaii identified him as a CPUSA member. What's more, anti-communist congressional committees, including the House Un-American Activities Committee (HUAC), accused Davis of involvement in several communist-front organizations.[40]

Obama writes about "Frank and his old Black Power dashiki self" giving him advice before he left for Occidental College in 1979 at the age of 18.[41]

Davis warned Obama not to "start believing what they tell you about equal opportunity and the American way and all that s---."[42]

The young Obama apparently took the advice to heart, as he relates in *Dreams from My Father:*

> To avoid being mistaken for a sellout, I chose my friends carefully. The more politically active black students. The foreign students. The Chícanos. The Marxist professors and structural feminists and punk rock performance poets.[43]

Once in Chicago after college:

> ... Obama became a "community organizer" and came into contact with more far-left political forces, including the Democratic Socialists of America, which maintains close ties to European socialist groups and parties through the Socialist International (SI), and two former members of the Students for a Democratic Society (SDS), William Ayers and Carl Davidson.[44]

Obama supporter Dr. Kathryn Takara, a professor of Interdisciplinary Studies at the University of Hawaii at Manoa, confirmed that Davis is the "Frank" in Obama's book. As Romerstein notes, she "did her dissertation on Davis and spent much time with him between 1972 until he passed away in 1987."[45]

In his article, "Communism in Hawaii and the Obama Connection," Cliff Kincaid writes:

> Obama's controversial former pastor, Jeremiah Wright, has strident anti-American views, links to such figures as Louis Farrakhan of the Nation of Islam, and has traveled to Cuba. But Frank Marshall Davis is a far more controversial figure because he was a member of the Soviet-controlled Communist Party USA (CPUSA). He was in Hawaii at the acknowledged suggestion of two other secret CPUSA members, actor Paul Robeson and labor leader Harry Bridges. Davis had been a writer for a CPUSA-controlled newspaper, the *Honolulu Record*.[46]

Among other things, Davis wrote a poem dedicated to the Soviet Red Army entitled "Smash on, victory-eating Red Army."[47]

He also wrote poems attacking traditional Christianity and the work of Christian missionaries.... One Davis poem, "Christ is a Dixie Nigger," dismisses Christ as "another New White Hope" and declares:

"Remember this, you wise guys
Your tales about Jesus of Nazareth are no-go with me
I've got a dozen Christs in Dixie all bloody and black...."[48]

CHICAGO TIES — THE WRIGHT STUFF

While at Harvard, Obama was an editor and then president of the *Harvard Law Review*, although he never published a single article under his name. Years later, an unsigned article by him published in 1990 in the review and advocating women's "reproductive" rights surfaced.[49]

The *Harvard Law Bulletin* noted that Obama was politically active, but rarely out front.

> By 1991, student protestors demanding that the school hire more black faculty had staged sit-ins inside the dean's office and filed a lawsuit alleging discrimination.
> Obama spoke at one protest rally, but largely preferred to stay behind the scenes and lead by example, recalls one of the protest leaders, Keith Boykin '92.[50]

Armed with a law degree, Obama moved to Chicago, where he became a law professor and community organizer in the mold of Saul Alinsky (1909-1972) and was tutored by Alinsky's disciples. *The Washington Post* reported that of Obama and Hillary Clinton:

> ...their common connection to Alinsky is one of the striking aspects of their biographies. Obama embraced many of Alinsky's tactics and recently said his years as an organizer gave him the best education of his life.[51]

Obama met his wife-to-be, Michelle Robinson, at a Chicago law firm, and they married in October 1992.

While in Chicago, Obama became active in left-wing circles, including the socialist New Party, which claimed him as a member and hailed his election as a state senator in its publications. The Spring 1996 *New Party News* endorsed

Obama's run for the state Senate and featured a photo of Obama with other leftists.[52] Trevor Loudon, the New Zealand blogger who broke the story on "Green Jobs Czar" Van Jones' communist background, in 2008 uncovered evidence of Obama's own radical ties in Chicago, and described the New Party:

> The New Party was the creation of the quasi-Marxist Democratic Socialists of America (DSA) and the radical community organisation ACORN. The Communist Party splinter group Committees of Correspondence (CoC) was also involved.[53]

Obama recalls that he was drawn to community organizing but had a problem of "authenticity." Raised by his white mother and his white maternal grandparents, Obama was looking for a way to demonstrate his "blackness." He found it by joining the Trinity United Church of Christ, pastored by Jeremiah Wright.

Reverend Jeremiah Wright
Zuma/Astrid Riecken

It was at Trinity that Obama recalls walking up the aisle and accepting Christ. Wright married Barack and Michelle, and baptized their two daughters, Malia and Natasha (Sasha). Obama has reportedly called Wright not just his pastor, but a friend and mentor as well.[54] Wright inspired the title of one of his two autobiographical books, *The Audacity of Hope* (2006).

For 20 years, Obama sat in the pews with his family and listened to Wright preach radical, race-centered Marxism dressed up in Christian clothing. As a minister in the United Church of Christ, Wright also supports his denomination's embrace of homosexuality and abortion "rights." But his main theme is black liberation theology.

For example, here is a snippet from a sermon Wright gave while boosting

Obama's candidacy and criticizing Hillary Clinton for being "rich" and "white":

> Jesus was a poor black man who lived in a country and in
> a culture that was controlled by rich white people.... We
> live in a culture that is controlled by and run by rich, white
> people. He taught me, Jesus did, how to love my enemies.
> Jesus taught me how to love the hell out of my enemies
> and not be reduced to their level of hatred, bigotry, and
> small-mindedness.[55]

Wright himself claims as a mentor James Cone, a Marxist who blends collectivism with Christian concepts. Here's a brief summary of the Wright/ Cone worldview, by Acton Research Institute Fellow Anthony B. Bradley:

> One of the pillars of Obama's home church, Trinity United
> Church of Christ, is "economic parity." On the website,
> Trinity claims that God is not pleased with "America's
> economic mal-distribution." Among all of controversial
> comments by Jeremiah Wright, the idea of massive wealth
> redistribution is the most alarming. The code language
> "economic parity" and references to "mal-distribution" is
> nothing more than channeling the twisted economic views
> of Karl Marx. Black Liberation theologians have explicitly
> stated a preference for Marxism as an ethical framework
> for the black church because Marxist thought is predicated
> on a system of oppressor class (whites) versus victim class
> (blacks).
> Black Liberation theologians James Cone and Cornel
> West have worked diligently to embed Marxist thought into
> the black church since the 1970s. For Cone, Marxism best
> addressed remedies to the condition of blacks as victims
> of white oppression. In *For My People*, Cone explains that
> "the Christian faith does not possess in its nature the
> means for analyzing the structure of capitalism. Marxism

as a tool of social analysis can disclose the gap between appearance and reality, and thereby help Christians to see how things really are."[56]

Wright's most famous gaffe occurred on the Sunday after 9/11, when he said in response to the terrorist attacks:

> We bombed Hiroshima, we bombed Nagasaki, and we nuked far more than the thousands in New York and the Pentagon, and we never batted an eye. We have supported state terrorism against the Palestinians and black South Africans, and now we are indignant because the stuff we have done overseas is now brought right back to our own front yards. America's chickens are coming home to roost.[57]

He also said:

> The government lied about inventing the HIV virus as a means of genocide against people of color. The government lied.[58]

And:

> The government gives them [African Americans] the drugs, builds bigger prisons, passes a three-strike law, and then wants us to sing "God Bless America." No, no, no. Not "God Bless America;" God damn America! That's in the Bible, for killing innocent people. God damn America for treating her citizen as less than human. God damn America as long as she keeps trying to act like she is God and she is supreme.[59]

Quicker than you can say Jeremiah Who?, the press lost interest in the presidential nominee's longtime pastor when these statements surfaced and conservative talk show hosts began reading them. Obama himself finally cut ties to Wright, denouncing some of Wright's more extreme comments.

Wright himself was quiet for a time, but then went public again, and essentially reiterated his most controversial remarks at an April 28, 2008, press conference at the National Press Club.[60] Here are some excerpts:

> MODERATOR: Jesus said, "I am the way, the truth, and the life. No man cometh unto the father but through me." Do you believe this? And do you think Islam is a way to salvation?

> WRIGHT: Jesus also said, "Other sheep have I who are not of this fold."

> (APPLAUSE)

> MODERATOR: Can you explain what you meant in a sermon shortly after 9/11 when you said the United States had brought the terrorist attacks on itself? Quote, "America's chickens are coming home to roost."

> WRIGHT: Have you heard the whole sermon? Have you heard the whole sermon?

> MODERATOR: I heard most of it.

> WRIGHT: No, no, the whole sermon, yes or no? No, you haven't heard the whole sermon? That nullifies that question.

> Well, let me try to respond in a non-bombastic way. If you heard the whole sermon, first of all, you heard that I was quoting the ambassador from Iraq. That's number one.

But, number two, to quote the Bible, "Be not deceived. God is not mocked. For whatsoever you sow, that you also shall reap." Jesus said, "Do unto others as you would have them do unto you."

You cannot do terrorism on other people and expect it never to come back on you. Those are biblical principles, not Jeremiah Wright bombastic, divisive principles.

As if any doubt remained as to Wright's radical leanings, he spoke at the Sept. 17, 2009, celebration of the 60th anniversary of the socialist magazine *Monthly Review*, where, after being introduced by self-avowed socialist Robert McChesney, founder of the far-left Free Press group that had communist Van Jones on its board, he praised the magazine for its "no-nonsense Marxism."[61]

He also described America as the "land of the greed and the home of the slave," and said of the *Monthly Review*:

You dispel all the negative images we have been programmed to conjure up with just the mention of that word socialism or Marxism.[62]

No wonder the media felt during the presidential campaign in 2008 that a guy like this, who had been Obama's pastor for 20 years, was not worth covering.

CHAPTER 2

AMERICA NOT CHRISTIAN, MAYBE MUSLIM

President Obama spent 20 years at Jeremiah Wright's Trinity United Church of Christ in Chicago and has said many times that he is a Christian. Since no one knows anyone's heart except the person and God Himself, we should take him at his word. But his actions before and since taking his oath as President raise questions about how he views his faith and how he views America.

Obama commented to French television on June 1, 2009, that the United States is "one of the largest Muslim countries in the world." Three days later, he gave an Islam-praising speech in Cairo, Egypt.

The CIA Factbook estimates America's Muslim population at 0.6 percent or about 1.8 million, which puts it in 58th place among nations with Muslims. Even if you take the Islamic Information Center's high estimate of 8 million, that still puts the U.S. at 29th out of 60 nations.[63]

In Cairo, Obama quoted from the Koran, used his middle name of Hussein, and indicated that the United States and Muslim nations have the same commitment to tolerance and freedom. To fathom the absurdity, think about the possibility of the Declaration of Independence and the U.S. Constitution springing from the pens of Islamic scholars Thomas al-Jefferson and James al-Madison.

In April, Obama bowed low to the Muslim king of Saudi Arabia, shocking many viewers who saw it on YouTube.[64]

Over the past three years, Obama has made it his business to insist that "we are no longer a Christian nation." He has said it in many places, here and abroad. In 2006, in Washington, D.C., he said,

> Whatever we once were, we are no longer a Christian nation. At least, not just.[65]

He posted the same sentiment on his campaign website.[66]

At the Compassion Forum at Messiah College in Pennsylvania on April 13, 2008, he said,

> We are not just a Christian nation. We are a Jewish nation; we are a Buddhist nation; we are a Muslim nation; Hindu nation; and we are a nation of atheists and nonbelievers.[67]

In Turkey, at a press conference on April 10, 2009, he said,

> Although we have a large Christian population, we do not consider ourselves a Christian nation or a Jewish nation or a Muslim nation. We consider ourselves a nation of citizens who are bound by ideals and a set of values. I think modern Turkey was founded with a similar set of values.[68]

During the presidential campaign, the media pounced on anyone who inquired into Obama's Muslim upbringing in Indonesia, his two Muslim fathers or his later 20-year attendance at radical pastor Jeremiah Wright's Trinity United Church of Christ in Chicago. Now, his Muslim roots are touted as an asset.

MOCKING THE BIBLE ON POLITICS

The media-enforced line for the past three years has been that Obama is a self-described mainstream Christian — end of story. Even when Obama badly distorted Jesus' Sermon on the Mount into a clarion call to accept homosexuality, the press yawned.[69] They yawned (or cheered) when he mocked the Bible's relevance for politics in that 2006 Washington, D.C., speech:

> Which passages of Scripture should guide our public policy? Should we go with Leviticus, which suggests slavery is okay? Or we could go with Deuteronomy, which suggests stoning your child if he strays from the faith, or should we just stick with the Sermon on the Mount, a passage which is so radical that it's doubtful that our own Defense Department would survive its application. Folks haven't been reading the Bible.[70]

More cheers came when he spoke the language of unity while taking a shot at his political opponents during a speech at the United Church of Christ convention in 2007:

> Somehow, somewhere along the way, faith stopped being used to bring us together and started being used to drive us apart. It got hijacked. Part of it's because of the so-called leaders of the Christian Right, who've been all too eager to exploit what divides us.
>
> We can recognize the truth that's at the heart of the UCC: that the conversation is not over [God needs an editor]; that our roles are not defined [men in dresses, unite]; that through ancient texts and modern voices, God is still speaking [yes, we're ripping out pages of the Bible daily to suit our appetites], challenging us to change not just our own lives, but the world around us ... hate has no

place in the hearts of believers.[71]

Question: Is it not hateful to suggest that people who disagree with you are full of "hate?" Is it unifying to accuse opponents of inventing fights that they didn't start?

Some more odd things occurred after Obama's election that should give pause to even the most cynical observers.

On the Saturday before Obama's swearing-in, V. Gene Robinson, the openly homosexual Episcopal bishop of New Hampshire, gave an invocation at a pre-inaugural event at the Lincoln Memorial. *The New York Times* interviewed him beforehand:

> Bishop Robinson said he had been rereading inaugural prayers through history and was "horrified" at how "specifically and aggressively Christian they were." Bishop Robinson said, "I am very clear that this will not be a Christian prayer, and I won't be quoting Scripture or anything like that. The texts that I hold as sacred are not sacred texts for all Americans, and I want all people to feel that this is their prayer."[72]

As one of his first judicial appointments, Obama named Indiana federal judge David Hamilton to the U.S. Seventh Circuit Court of Appeals. Hamilton, who had ruled that a pastor could not invoke the name of Jesus in an opening prayer for the Indiana legislature, said that, on the other hand, invoking Allah at a public event is fine.[73]

In April, it was reported that Obama appointed Harry Knox, a Catholic-bashing homosexual activist, to the Advisory Council on Faith-Based and Neighborhood Partnerships. Knox, who directs the religion program at the largest gay pressure group, the Human Rights Campaign, described Pope Benedict and other Catholic clergy as "discredited leaders" because of their stand for traditional marriage, and called the Knights of Columbus "foot soldiers of a discredited army of oppression" because of their support of California's Proposition 8 marriage amendment.[74]

On April 14, 2009, the Obama team had Georgetown University cover up the Greek letters IHS, which stand for Jesus, so they would not show up when he spoke in front of them.[75]

NO TO NATIONAL DAY OF PRAYER

On May 7, 2009, Obama declined to hold any White House event to mark the National Day of Prayer, a decision hailed by Barry Lynn's hard left Americans United for the Separation of Church and State.[76] On September 1, 2009, however, he hosted an *iftar* dinner to mark the Muslim holy month of Ramadan, something his predecessor, George Bush, had also done.[77]

In his eloquent commencement speech at Notre Dame on May 17, 2009, Obama sounded a conciliatory note, lamented, sort of, the abortions that he wants taxpayers to fund, and gave more clues that Christianity will move over and shrink before a universalist moral relativism:

> The size and scope of the challenges before us require that we remake [not "reform" or "restore," but "remake"] our world to renew its promise; that we align our deepest values and commitments to the demands of a new age.
>
> Your generation must decide how to save God's creation from a changing climate that threatens to destroy it.... And we must find a way to reconcile our ever-shrinking world with its ever-growing diversity – diversity of thought, diversity of culture, and diversity of belief.[78]
> [*italic editorial note added*]

If diversity in and of itself is god, where does that leave Jesus Christ – the Lord of Lords and King of Kings, the Alpha and the Omega, the Way, the Truth and the Life, through Whom all things were created?

Well, the Obama team might just ask Him to change his name to ... Allah.[79]

A GLIMPSE AT OBAMA'S LEGISLATIVE RECORD ON ABORTION

1997 — As an Illinois state senator, Obama votes against SB 230, a bill that would have banned the barbaric procedure known as partial birth abortion.[80]

2001 — Obama is the lone Illinois senator to take the floor to oppose a bill that would have mandated medical care for babies born after botched abortions. Obama says that if a nine-month-old baby who survived a late-term, labor-induced abortion is considered to be a person who had a right to live, the law would outlaw abortions.[81]

2002 — Obama votes against another "born alive" bill (SB 1661) that would have held a doctor accountable if the doctor harmed, neglected or failed to provide care for a child born alive after an unsuccessful abortion.[82]

2003 — On March 12, SB 1082, another state bill identical to the federal Infant Born Alive Protection Act, is killed in the committee chaired by Obama, who himself votes to kill it.[83]

Obama explained his "born alive" votes in 2008 on his own Website, Organizing for America:

> Whenever we define a pre-viable fetus as a person that is protected by the equal protection clause or other elements of the Constitution, we're saying they are persons entitled to the kinds of protections provided to a child, a 9-month-old child delivered to term.... That determination then essentially, if it was accepted by a court,

would forbid abortions to take place.[84]

Douglas Johnson of the National Right to Life Committee comments:

> The Obama of 2001-2003 really did object to a bill merely because it defended the proposition, "A live child born as a result of an abortion shall be fully recognized as a human person and accorded immediate protection under the law." And it is that reality that he now desperately wants to conceal from the eyes of the public.[85]

Pro-life nurse Jill Stanek explains how Obama tried to escape the implications of his 2003 vote against the Illinois version of the Born Alive Infants Protection Act:

> For 4 years following his 2003 vote Obama misrepresented it, stating the wording of the Illinois version of Born Alive was not the same as the federal version, and he would have voted for it if so. As recently as August 16, 2008 Obama made this false assertion.

> But when evidence presented was irrefutable, Obama's campaign on August 18, 2008, admitted the truth to the *New York Sun*.

> The nonpartisan group *FactCheck.org* has since corroborated Obama voted against identical legislation as passed overwhelmingly on the federal level and then misrepresented

his vote.[86]

2006 – U.S. Sen. Obama votes against the Child Interstate Abortion Notification Act (S.403), a bill prohibiting minor girls from being taken across state lines without parental consent to have an abortion in circumvention of the laws of 45 states which require parental consent or notification in order for a minor to have an abortion.[87]

2007 – On May 11, U.S. Sen. Obama co-sponsors the Freedom of Choice Act, a measure to eliminate all state and federal restrictions on abortion.[88]

2007 – On July 17, Obama promises the Planned Parenthood Action Fund to put federally funded abortion "at the heart" of his government health care takeover plan:

> In my mind, reproductive care is essential care.
> It is basic care, so it is at the center and at the
> heart of the plan that I propose.[89]

2007 – Pro-abortion lobby NARAL gives Obama his third consecutive 100 percent rating for his Senate voting record.[90]

CHAPTER 3

OBAMA'S INSPIRATION: SAUL ALINSKY

The Obama campaign used the glitzy and heavily staged 2008 Democratic National Convention to successfully showcase the junior senator from Illinois to the nation. The political gathering climaxed with a grand stadium rally, complete with faux Greek columns, at which 75,000 ecstatic fans cheered Obama's acceptance speech.

Much of Obama's success came courtesy of the ideas and influence of social activist Saul Alinksy. The tactics employed at the convention were the result of "Barack Obama's training in Chicago by the great community organizers," according to David Alinsky, whose father, Saul, devised a methodology for social action that Obama learned in Chicago.

"[T]he method of my late father always works to get the message out and get the supporters on board," Alinsky's son wrote. "When executed meticulously and thoughtfully, it is a powerful strategy for initiating change and making it really happen. Obama learned his lesson well."[91]

GIVING CREDIT TO LUCIFER

The elder Alinsky laid out those lessons in 1971, in his book called *Rules for Radicals: A Pragmatic Primer for Realistic Radicals.*[92] A "community organizer" since at least the 1920s, Alinsky had schooled countless young idealistic reformers in the arts of obtaining political power in order to promote various left-wing causes.

Published a year before Alinsky's death in 1972, the book begins with quotes from a rabbi, then Thomas Paine, and finally Alinsky himself, who wrote:

> Lest we forget at least an over-the-shoulder acknowledgement to the very first radical: from all our legends, mythology, and history (and who is to know where mythology leaves off and history begins — or which is which). The first radical known to man who rebelled against the establishment and did it so effectively that he at least won his own kingdom — Lucifer.[93]

That's right. Alinsky saluted Satan as his inspiration.

And a devilish business it is since Alinsky's primer is all about using deception, manipulation and raw power to bring about a communist future.

Rules for Radicals is a blueprint for organizing. Most of what Alinksy says is common sense and politically astute. His methods would aid anyone who wants to organize for a cause. The problem is that he begins with a flawed premise: relativism in the service of Marxism.

"All values and factors are relative," he states in the prologue (p. xv). He imagines "the young" of today writing the Declaration of Independence, beginning with the phrase "When in the course of inhuman events...." After listing a litany of social ills, from war to hate to poverty, he says "such a bill of particulars would emphasize the absurdity of human affairs and the forlornness and emptiness, the fearful loneliness that comes from not knowing if there is any meaning to our lives" (p. xvii).

Like any good Marxist, he returns to the theme of "alienation" of the masses and emphasizes that only power matters and that alliances and causes shift to reflect the realities of power: "All of life is partisan." Elsewhere, he writes, "ethical standards must be elastic to stretch with the times" (p. 30).

"An organizer working in and for an open society is in an ideological dilemma. To begin with, he does not have a fixed truth — truth to him is relative and changing: *everything* to him is relative and changing. He is a political relativist" (p. 11).

Saul Alinsky
AP

He goes on to state that an organizer is "loose, resilient, fluid" and "in the end, he has one conviction — a belief that if people have the power to act, in the long run they will, most of the time, reach the right decisions." He is quite aware that he has just violated his belief in relativism, but rationalizes it this way: "I am not concerned if this faith in people is regarded as a prime truth and therefore a contradiction of what I have already written, for life is a story of contradictions" (p. 11). He continues that theme throughout the book — that one can and must break any rule as long as it advances your goal. As Marx wrote, "the ends justify the means."

Much of the time, Mr. Alinsky sounds like a slightly cynical but essentially good advocate of self-government. But keep in mind that he put these concepts to work for causes and organizations that relentlessly expanded government power. "Power to the people" is one of the surest paths to power for an ambitious leader.

America's founders had a more cautionary view of human character based on Christian insight into man's fallen nature, which is why they spent so much time figuring out ways to limit government. Unlike Alinsky and other leftists, they believed that people, although created in the image of God, are not basically good. We're all sinners whether we like it or not, and must fight daily against overweening selfishness. Hence, the founders built a system to contain and curb the consequences of human flaws while allowing maximum freedom. They knew that self-interest is not bad and can produce many good things, but it can become tyrannical unless tempered by belief in a God of justice and mercy.

GOOD INTENTIONS, RADICAL RISKS

The Left, in the name of freedom, cedes more and more power to the government in the hopes that government will not become oppressive and that self-interest can be subordinated to the good of all. All totalitarian regimes, from the Nazis to the Communists, always begin with stated good intentions and the promise that they will improve the human race and its living conditions. But here's the catch: Any government with enough power to radically change people's lives has the power to radically worsen them as well.

Saul Alinsky spent much of his time training others to organize minorities and the poor to increase their power. This is a noble goal, except when these same poor people become pawns to the ambitions of a few who rise to power in an expanding state. In the Communist Manifesto, Karl Marx described the elites who would lead as the "vanguard" in the "dictatorship of the proletariat." Organizers, Alinsky said, regard themselves as the vanguard, driven not by power, per se, but "by the desire to create. The organizer is in a true sense reaching for the highest level for which man can reach — to create, to be a 'great creator,' to play God" (p. 61).

This is strikingly similar to what the devil offered Eve: "Ye shall be like God, knowing good and evil" (Genesis 3:5). But while Alinsky the Organizer saw Satan as a liberator, the Bible gives a profoundly different view:

> Be sober, be vigilant; because your adversary the devil walks about like a roaring lion, seeking whom he may devour (I Peter 5:8).
>
> And they had as king over them the angel of the bottomless pit, whose name in Hebrew is Abaddon, but in Greek he has the name Apollyon (Revelation 9:11).

Both Abaddon and Apollyon mean "destroyer."

CHAPTER 4

ACORN AND OBAMA

The Association of Community Organizations for Reform Now (ACORN) is, according to researcher/writer Sol Stern, "the largest radical group in the country."[94] We're taking a look at it here, since Barack Obama worked closely with it as a trainer, attorney, and organizer in the early to mid-1990s.

Even before ACORN employees were caught in a 2009 video sting operation offering advice on how to cheat on taxes and operate houses of prostitution with trafficked underage girls, ACORN was developing a reputation as a hard Left group that bent the rules and used hardball tactics to battle "capitalism" and "empower" the poor through bigger government.

VOTER FRAUD

In 2008, ACORN faced accusations in more than a dozen states that it had illegally registered to vote thousands of dead people, celebrities, and cartoon characters such as Donald Duck and Minnie Mouse. ACORN has championed "Motor Voter" registration, which critics say is a ticket to voter fraud. As an attorney, Barack Obama represented ACORN in an Illinois "Motor Voter" case, as noted by the *Wall Street Journal's* John Fund:

> In 1995, then GOP Gov. Jim Edgar refused to implement the federal "Motor Voter" law. Allowing voters to register using only a postcard and blocking the state from culling voter rolls, he argued, could invite fraud. Mr. Obama sued on behalf of the Association of Community Organizations for Reform Now, and won. Acorn later invited Mr. Obama to help train its staff; Mr. Obama would also sit on the board of the Woods Fund for Chicago, which frequently gave this group grants.[95]

Fund further notes that:

> In Seattle, local officials invalidated 1,762 Acorn registrations. Felony charges were filed against seven of its workers, some of whom have criminal records. Prosecutors say Acorn's oversight of its workers was virtually nonexistent. To avoid prosecution, Acorn agreed to pay $25,000 in restitution.
>
> Despite this record — and polls that show clear majorities of blacks and Hispanics back voter ID laws — Mr. Obama continues to back Acorn. They both joined briefs urging the Supreme Court to overturn Indiana's law.[96]

ACORN has also specialized in "shaking down" financial institutions, in which banks are told that they will be portrayed by the media as racists and bigots unless they lend to people who can't afford to pay back the loans. The result: millions of bad loans resulting in foreclosures and astronomical debt. Several congressmen are demanding an investigation into ACORN's role in the 2008 housing market collapse, which led to the nation's financial meltdown.

In 2003, Sol Stern wrote an eye-opening exposé of ACORN in *City Journal:*

ACORN has 120,000 dues-paying members, chapters in 700 poor neighborhoods in 50 cities, and 30 years' experience. It promotes a 1960s-bred agenda of anti-capitalism, central planning, victimology, and government handouts to the poor. As a result, not only does it harm the poor it claims to serve; it is also a serious threat to the urban future.

It is no surprise that ACORN preaches a New Left-inspired gospel, since it grew out of one of the New Left's silliest and most destructive groups, the National Welfare Rights Organization (NWRO). In the mid-sixties, founder George Wiley forged an army of tens of thousands of single minority mothers, whom he sent out to disrupt welfare offices through sit-ins and demonstrations demanding an end to the "oppressive" eligibility restrictions that kept down the welfare rolls. His aim: to flood the welfare system with so many clients that it would burst, creating a crisis that, he believed, would force a radical restructuring of America's unjust capitalist economy.

The flooding succeeded beyond Wiley's wildest dreams. From 1965 to 1974, the number of single-parent households on welfare soared from 4.3 million to 10.8 million, despite mostly flush economic times. By the early 1970s, one person was on the welfare rolls in New York City for every two working in the city's private economy.[97]

New York City declared bankruptcy in 1975.

CREATING CRISIS

The tactics of the NWRO and its successor ACORN reflect a radical plan now known as the Cloward-Piven Strategy.[98] DiscoveringtheNetworks.org, a website run by former Leftist David Horowitz, and which specializes in exposing the political Left, explains:

First proposed in 1966 and named after Columbia University sociologists Richard Andrew Cloward and Frances Fox Piven, the "Cloward-Piven Strategy" seeks to hasten the fall of capitalism by overloading the government bureaucracy with a flood of impossible demands, thus pushing society into crisis and economic collapse....

Rather than placating the poor with government hand-outs, wrote Cloward and Piven, activists should work to sabotage and destroy the welfare system; the collapse of the welfare state would ignite a political and financial crisis that would rock the nation; poor people would rise in revolt; only then would "the rest of society" accept their demands.

The key to sparking this rebellion would be to expose the inadequacy of the welfare state. Cloward-Piven's early promoters cited radical organizer Saul Alinsky as their inspiration.[99]

Cloward and Piven not only wrote about revolution but recruited Wiley to lead the new movement. On September 27, 1970, *The New York Times* reported that Wiley's National Welfare Rights Organization (which morphed into ACORN) employed many disruptive tactics, including "sit-ins in legislative chambers, including a United States Senate committee hearing, mass demonstrations of several thousand welfare recipients, school boycotts, picket lines, mounted police, tear gas, arrests – and, on occasion, rock-throwing, smashed glass doors, overturned desks, scattered papers and ripped-out phones."[100]

The tactics worked, and major institutions buckled under the pressure to expand welfare. It wasn't until 1996 that Congress managed to enact major welfare reform following a plan championed by Ronald Reagan's California "Welfare Reform Czar," Robert B. Carleson.[101] Over the next few years, millions were freed from welfare dependence.

Fast forward to February 17, 2009. President Obama signs a $787 billion stimulus bill that has a major, virtually unreported provision: repealing the

1996 welfare reform.[102] This was followed by billions more in spending.

In December 2009, the Obama Administration and Congress agreed to raise the federal debt ceiling past $12 trillion, with leading Democrats saying the ceiling would have to be raised again by early 2010.[103] They sure did. On January 28, they raised the ceiling by $1.9 trillion to bring up the federal debt limit to $14.4 trillion.[104]

And on March 23, 2010, ignoring polls showing a large majority opposing it, Obama signed into law the government takeover of the nation's health care system, which included a federal takeover of college student loan programs. The 2,733-page bill will cost as much as $2.3 trillion over the next decade, impose numerous new taxes, create dozens of new federal agencies and increase the size of the Internal Revenue Service to enforce it. The bill contains an unconstitutional mandate for individuals to purchase government-approved health insurance or face fines or jail. If not repealed, the health care takeover will change the fundamental relationship of American citizens to their government, making them dependent on the goodwill of federal bureaucrats for their families' health and even their lives in some cases.

PART 2

RADICALS IN POWER

CHAPTER 5

RAHM EMANUEL
CHIEF OF STAFF

Rahm Emanuel, 50, epitomizes "Chicago Style" machine politics in which rules are broken and people threatened or pampered as needed to ensure support. He is a practitioner of bare-knuckle tactics and famously said, "You don't ever want a crisis to go to waste. It's an opportunity to do things that you would otherwise avoid."[105]

Although the media dubbed him a "centrist" upon his being named chief of staff, his voting record as an Illinois congressman from 2003 to 2008 was clearly on the far left. The American Conservative Union gave him an overall 13 out of 100 and an outright 0 rating in 2007, while the liberal Americans for Democratic Action gave him a 96 percent overall rating, as reported by the Media Research Center's Tim Graham.[106]

Even more revealing, the National Abortion Rights Action League (NARAL) gave Emanuel a 100 percent rating, while the National Right to Life Committee gave him a zero. He voted:

- No on banning partial-birth abortion;
- No on barring the transport of minors across state lines for abortions;
- No on making it a crime to harm a fetus during another crime;
- Yes on expanding embryonic stem cell research;
- No on forbidding human cloning for research purposes.[107]

Emanuel is also 100 percent pro-homosexual, as evidenced by his 100 percent voting record as scored by the largest homosexual pressure group, the Human Rights Campaign.[108] Emanuel voted Yes on the Employment Non-Discrimination Act (ENDA) and No on the constitutional amendment protecting marriage as the union of one man and one woman. He also co-sponsored a bill giving marital benefits to domestic partners of federal employees and co-sponsored a bill re-introducing the radical feminist Equal Rights Amendment.[109]

FIERY AND PROFANE

Emanuel is a study in contrasts, according to observers. He is urbane, intelligent, and is even a ballet dancer, but he has a fiery temper and a foul mouth. In a 2008 article assessing the new chief of staff, *Newsweek*'s Susan Smalley and Evan Thomas wrote:

> Rahm Emanuel has been described as a street fighter with a killer instinct — as explosive, profane, wired and ruthless — sometimes as a compliment, sometimes not.... In conversation with almost anyone about anything, Emanuel uses the F word like a sergeant in a World War II motor pool.[110]

Emanuel has been a mainstay of liberal Democratic activism almost his entire adult life. Beginning on Illinois Sen. Paul Simon's Senate re-election campaign in 1984, he quickly moved up the ranks as a top Democratic fundraiser until 1991, when he joined the nascent presidential campaign of then-Governor Bill Clinton. Emanuel demanded the controversial strategy of focusing on national fundraising rather than local events in New Hampshire, as other candidates were doing. Eventually, Clinton's massive war chest, courtesy of Emanuel, enabled him to survive the Gennifer Flowers "bimbo explosion" scandal, carry Super Tuesday and cruise to the nomination.

Rahm Emanuel
Zuma/Michael Reynolds

Emanuel's reaction to the victory? At a dinner party in Little Rock for senior staff the night after the election, "as about a score of them sat around a picnic table mushily declaring their love for one another, Emanuel picked up a knife and called out the names of different politicians who had '*expletive deleted* us.' After each name, Emanuel would cry out, 'Dead man!'—and stab the knife into the table," according to *Chicago Tribune* reporter Naftali Bendavid.[111]

The politicians in question included Democrats who had committed the cardinal sin of supporting other candidates in the primaries. "'When he was done, the table looked like a lunar landscape,' one campaign veteran recalls. 'It was like something out of *The Godfather*. But that's Rahm for you,'" according to *Rolling Stone* magazine, which described Emanuel as "the political brains of Bill Clinton's White House."[112]

DEAD FISH DELIVERY

Washington politicians have learned to beware the wrath of Rahm, or "Rahmbo" as he is often known. This is, after all, the man who "sent a pollster who was late delivering polling results a dead fish in a box," according to *Newsweek*[113] and the *New York Times*.[114] He is arguably the most important person in the Obama White House after the President himself.

Emanuel's reputation for staff abuse is legendary. When he was a senior advisor in the Clinton White House, Hillary Clinton tried to fire him in 1993, "reportedly because he was too abrasive with others," according to *Newsweek*.[115] He refused to leave unless the order came from President Clinton directly, which it never did.

During the 1998 Presidential impeachment, as British Prime Minister Tony Blair was preparing a pro-Clinton speech, he "reportedly screamed to Blair's face 'Don't *expletive* this up!' while Clinton was present; Blair and Clinton both burst into laughter," according to Con Coughlin in his 2006 book *American Ally: Tony Blair and the War on Terror*.[116]

But with his wrath comes a clear effectiveness. Longtime Clinton aide Bruce Reed described Emanuel as "a realist. He's honest, he tells it like it is. Rahm is extraordinarily good at getting things done. ... [He is] an acquired taste. I always tease him that those of us who don't hate him love him a lot." Another Clinton staffer, Paul Begala, praised him saying, "The Democratic Party is full of Rhodes Scholars — Rahm is a road warrior. He's just what the Democrats need to fight back."[117]

During the George W. Bush administration, Emanuel returned to his native Chicago, where in 2002 he was elected to Congress, succeeding Rod Blagojevich upon Blagojevich's election as Governor. Blagojevich was eventually forced to resign amid a financial scandal. Emanuel very quickly ascended to the chairmanship of the Democratic Congressional Campaign Committee (DCCC), where he was the member of the Democratic Party most responsible for taking control of the House of Representatives in the 2006 elections. They did so due in no small part to his fundraising and recruitment abilities.

Following the 2008 Election, where the Democrats increased their control of the House, Emanuel went to the Obama White House where he quickly became, in the words of *The New York Times*, "perhaps the most influential chief of staff in a generation." In this position, he leaves the ideology to the President while he focuses on turning the ideology into political reality.

CHAPTER 6

VAN JONES
"GREEN JOBS CZAR"

O n April 6, 2009, New Zealand blogger Trevor Loudon broke the story[118] that Obama's "green jobs czar" Van Jones, author of the 2008 bestseller *The Green Collar Economy*, had a communist background.[119]

Four months later, on September 6, after Fox News Channel talk show host Glenn Beck spent two weeks revealing to a wider audience Jones' radical connections, Jones became the first major figure to resign from the Obama Administration.

A longstanding radical lawyer, Jones, 41, had decided that the best way to bring about a Marxist revolution in America and the world was by repainting the movement from red to green and using environmentalism as the tool to build a socialist society. If all things were related to carbon's impact on the environment, including CO_2, the very air we exhale, then the government would have to get into every nook and cranny of people's lives.

As "green jobs czar," Jones had at his disposal $60 billion in Troubled Asset Relief Program (TARP) funds to spend on creating eco-friendly jobs. But

Van Jones
Newscom

he didn't get far before his radical past caught up with him. Between Loudon, Glenn Beck, WorldNetDaily.com, Accuracy in Media, and more in the blogosphere, a mountain of dirt was piling up about Jones that finally could not be ignored. The question arose: how could such a certifiably extreme left-winger be appointed to a White House position?

On September 7, the *Washington Post* ran this headline exculpating President Obama from selecting Jones as his "Green Jobs Czar": "In Adviser's Resignation, Vetting Bites Obama."[120]

The article quotes an anonymous White House official who said that "Jones' past was not studied as intensively as that of other advisers because of his relatively low rank." Jones did not require Senate confirmation.

A far more likely explanation is that the Obama team knew full well what Jones was about and saw no problem. As a disciple of radical community organizer Saul Alinsky, why would Obama recoil from a man who was using Alinsky's methods to a T? Besides, evidence abounds that the White House was fully aware of Jones' past.

Fox's Beck ran tape of White House Senior Advisor Valerie Jarrett boasting that they had been watching Jones' activities for years and finally "were so delighted to recruit him into the White House."[121]

MEDIA IGNORE CONTROVERSY

From the *Washington Post* to the *Los Angeles Times*, to the TV networks and news magazines, the media ignored the growing controversy over Jones' communist background as it built over a two-week period prior to his resignation. Beck led the charge, along with Breitbart.com and blogs such as Gateway Pundit, which broke the story about Jones being a 9/11 "truther."

The "truthers" are the people in tinfoil hats who say the Bush Administration either knew about the attacks beforehand or was actually complicit. The *New York Times* did not cover any of this until Jones resigned on September. 6.

At the schizophrenic *Wall Street Journal*, the truth-telling editorial page noted on September 8 that Jones "has been a leading young light of the left-wing political movement for many years" with a "long trail of extreme comments and left-wing organizations."[122] Meanwhile, reporters over on the news page blamed "the right" and said Jones "resigned after conservatives seized on a series of controversial statements."[123]

Jones, who had moved to Los Angeles in 1992 to join a leftist lawyers group that was monitoring the trial of police officers in the Rodney King riots, was among those arrested in riots that followed the not guilty verdicts. In jail, he became even more radicalized.

The East Bay Express reports how Jones devised a way to channel his Marxism into an environmental engine, and quotes Jones as saying:

> "I met all these young radical people of color — I mean really radical, communists and anarchists. And it was, like, 'This is what I need to be a part of.'" Although he already had a plane ticket, he decided to stay in San Francisco. "I spent the next ten years of my life working with a lot of those people I met in jail, trying to be a revolutionary." In the months that followed, he let go of any lingering thoughts that he might fit in with the status quo. "I was a rowdy nationalist on April 28th, and then the verdicts came down on April 29th," he said. "By August, I was a communist."[124]

When his number was up at the White House on September 6, Jones did not exactly go quietly. His written statement says that "opponents of reform have mounted a vicious smear campaign against me. They are using lies and distortions to distract and divide." Well, for it to be a smear or lie, it's got to be inaccurate. Even the drive-by media have finally reported the ugly facts about

Jones' involvement with the "truthers," and as a founder of the now-disbanded Bay Area communist group Standing Together to Organize a Revolutionary Movement (STORM).

The *Post* delicately describes STORM as having "Marxist roots." Yes, and trunk and branches and fruit. *Reclaiming Revolution*, a history of the organization published in 2004, relates that it was an outgrowth of the early '90s group Roots Against War (RAW), which "laid the groundwork for the next decade of revolutionary politics among young people of color in the Bay Area"[125] (p. 5). A quick analysis is available on the website of Reformed evangelical conservative David Westerfield.[126] After RAW disbanded in 1992, the activists reformed as STORM in 1994, with "a political commitment to the fundamental ideas of Marxism-Leninism" (p. 51). STORM disbanded in December 2002.

Here's more from Accuracy in Media's Cliff Kincaid:

> Jones was deeply involved in a Marxist group, Standing Together To Organize a Revolutionary Movement (STORM), which sent some of its members to Cuba for brainwashing. Jones was also on a list of "veteran activists" attending a conference in the summer of 1998 at the University of Illinois at Chicago, the same place where Weather Underground leader Bill Ayers is now a professor, in order to plot the "Black Liberation Agenda for the 21st Century" under the auspices of the Black Radical Congress. Angela Davis, former Communist Party USA official, participated, and the CPUSA helped organize the event. Jones named a son in honor of Amilcar Cabral, the African Marxist.
>
> CAP insisted that Jones had renounced his communist views in 2000 and favored "business-based solutions" for the environment. But, in fact, he gave an interview last year to "Uprising Radio" stating that his goals were "transforming the whole society" and going beyond "systems of exploitation and oppression" and even

"eco-capitalism."[127]

BLAMING AMERICA FOR 9/11

Jones was a speaker at an Oakland rally on September 12, 2001, that blamed the U.S. itself for bringing on the September 11 terror attacks and warned that the Arab-American community faced "a tidal wave of bigotry."[128] As Scott Johnson of the Powerline blog reported:

> Jones said, "The bombs the government drops in Iraq are the bombs that blew up in New York City. The U.S. cannot bomb its way out of this one. Safety at home requires justice abroad."
>
> That's what Jones had to say while the ruins still smoldered and bodies had yet to be removed from the rubble.[129]

In 1999, Jones led a campaign demanding the release of convicted cop killer and avowed communist Mumia Abu-Jamal, who had shot a police officer in the face.[130] And he has joined other communist-led protests against law enforcers, as reported by *The Washington Times*:

> [Jones'] name is posted online in support of an October 2006 petition[131] to stop police brutality posted by the *Revolution* newspaper, which describes itself as the "Voice of the Revolutionary Communist Party, USA." The petition was created by a group called the October 22nd Coalition that seeks to "meet the intensifying nationwide epidemic of police brutality with resistance on the national level" and says it works with the International Concerned Family and Friends of Mumia Abu Jamal.
>
> Other groups and individuals signing the petition include: Act Now to Stop War and End Racism, Freedom Socialist Party of San Francisco, International Socialist Organization of San Francisco, Justice4Palestinians, New

Black Panther Party's New York Chapter and the Party for Socialism and Liberation.[132]

Peter Ferrara, who served in the White House Office of Policy Development under President Reagan and who is now General Counsel for the American Civil Rights Union, wrote in the *American Spectator:*

> Jones explained his job as White House green jobs czar by saying, "This movement is deeper than a solar panel! Deeper than a solar panel! Don't stop there! Don't stop there! We're going to change the whole system! We're going to change the whole thing. We want a new system. We want a new system." This statement is especially troubling coming from a self-avowed communist radical with extensive ties to other communist revolutionaries. What new system would he be talking about, and is that what those who voted for Obama last year thought they were supporting?
>
> Jones has also publicly alleged that under our capitalist agricultural system, Americans are spraying immigrants with poisonous toxins. He said:
>
> "What about our immigrant brothers and sisters? What about people who come here from all around the world who we're willing to have out in the field, with poison being sprayed on them, poison being sprayed on them because we have the wrong agricultural system."
>
> Jones has also called for redistribution of wealth to American Indians, saying, "No more broken treaties, no more broken treaties. Give them the wealth! Give them the wealth!"[133]

One of the less important charges against Jones was his public use of the a-word to describe Republicans who are resisting the health care takeover. The Left routinely uses foul language, so this unwise remark should not have come as a surprise.

But all in all, it added up to an embarrassing array of revelations that were simply too much for the Obama Administration to depend on the mainstream media to cover up. Jones finally had to go.

CHAPTER 7

MARK LLOYD
"DIVERSITY CZAR" AT THE FCC

A longtime left-wing activist, Lloyd was appointed as the "diversity czar" on July 29, 2009 at the Federal Communications Commission (FCC), the agency that regulates broadcast radio and television and is beginning to regulate the Internet.

Lloyd, who worked for CNN and NBC, most recently handled media and telecom issues as a Vice President for Strategic Initiatives at the liberal Leadership Conference on Civil Rights/Education Fund, and was also a board member of the left-leaning Benton Foundation,[134] which is lobbying Congress to draft an Internet regulation plan.

Lloyd's official title at the FCC is Associate General Counsel and Chief Diversity Officer. His main job, to put it bluntly, is to remove from radio management white males, who tend to be more conservative, and replace them with minorities, homosexuals and women. His specific duties were revealed after the conservative group Judicial Watch received an answer on November 12, 2009, to its Freedom of Information Act request.[135]

PRAISE FOR CHAVEZ

Lloyd's political views came into sharp focus, when, on June 10, 2008, at the National Conference for Media Reform (NCMR) in Minneapolis, Lloyd discussed Venezuelan dictator Hugo Chavez. An anti-American Fidel Castro ally who has seized private property in Venezuela, referred to President George Bush as the "devil" in a United Nations speech, shut down dissenting media, and is working to turn Venezuela and all of South America communist, Chavez was praised by Lloyd as follows:

> In Venezuela, with Chavez, is really an incredible revolution – a democratic revolution, to begin to put in place things that are going to have an impact on the people of Venezuela.
>
> The property owners and the folks who then controlled the media in Venezuela rebelled – worked, frankly, with folks here in the U.S. government – worked to oust him. But he came back with another revolution, and then Chavez began to take very seriously the media in his country.[136]

Very seriously. Chavez shut down more than 30 radio stations that had dared criticize him, and threatened to close the major opposition TV station. The video footage of Lloyd's remarks in Minnesota was uncovered on Fox News Channel's *Glenn Beck Show* on August 26, 2009.[137]

The Media Research Center's Communications Director, Seton Motley, who heads that group's opposition to reinstatement of the Fairness Doctrine, writes:

> Lloyd is in fact a Saul Alinsky disciple. In his 2006 book entitled *Prologue to a Farce: Communication and Democracy in America*, he calls for an all-out "confrontational movement" against private media. He wants leftist activists – through incessant political pressure – and the government – through the creation

of a totally untenable operating environment of fees, fines and regulations — to work together to force the commercial broadcasters out, to be replaced by public broadcasters.[138]

In *Prologue*, Lloyd shared his jaundiced view about First Amendment freedoms:

It should be clear by now that my focus here is not freedom of speech or the press. This freedom is all too often an exaggeration. At the very least, blind references to freedom of speech or the press serve as a distraction from the critical examination of other communications policies.

[T]he purpose of free speech is warped to protect global corporations and block rules that would promote democratic governance.[139]

FROM MEDIA REFORM TO SOCIALISM

As a Senior Fellow at the Center for American Progress (CAP), Lloyd co-wrote a June 2007 report with authors from another left-wing group, the Free Press, entitled "The Structural Imbalance of Political Talk Radio."[140] The Free Press was co-founded by avowed Marxist Robert McChesney and had fellow communist Van Jones on its board until he resigned in 2008. As Accuracy in Media reports:

In an article in the socialist *Monthly Review*, "Journalism, Democracy, and Class Struggle," McChesney declared, "Our job is to make media reform part of our broader struggle for democracy, social justice, and, dare we say it, socialism."[141]

McChesney introduced Obama's former pastor, Jeremiah Wright, at an anniversary celebration of the *Review* on September 17, 2009.[142] Wright

Mark Lloyd
joebeone

praised the *Review*'s "no-nonsense Marxism."[143]

Lloyd's book and the CAP report argue for forcing private broadcasters to heavily subsidize public broadcasting.[144] The CAP report, which cooks the stats by, among other things, ignoring the left-leaning massive National Public Radio network, complains that the success of conservative talk radio hosts such as Rush Limbaugh represents a failure of freedom of speech that the government must correct.

The report asserts that conservatives control 91 percent of talk radio, with "progressives" controlling a mere 9 percent. Even if this were true, which is doubtful, liberals control the rest of America's major media, including the TV broadcast networks and cable networks (except for Fox), newspapers, news magazines and commercial radio news outlets.[145] The only major medium dominated by conservatives is talk radio. (Even though cable's Fox News Channel has nine of the 10 top news and commentary programs, Fox has fewer overall viewers than the combined totals of CNN, CNN Headline News and MSNBC.)[146]

Lloyd and his co-authors want a return to the Fairness Doctrine, the federal rule that had prevented the development of a robust talk radio market until it was discontinued in 1987 under President Reagan.[147] But since public pressure has persuaded Congress that reviving the Fairness Doctrine would be highly unpopular, the report recommends a back-door approach, achieving the same thing through three policies that would increase "localism" and "diversity" of ownership and content. The boldface headers below are verbatim from the report.

1) **"Restore local and national caps on the ownership of commercial radio stations"** (p. 9). This would effectively break up the companies that

provide nationally syndicated programs with such hosts as Rush Limbaugh, Sean Hannity, Michael Savage, Laura Ingraham and Mark Levin.

2) **"Ensure greater local accountability over radio licensing"** (p. 10). The first recommendation under this heading is to limit licenses to only three years, and force station owners to go through a rigorous re-authorization process. Imagine local broadcasting boards stacked with "community organizers" from ACORN demanding more local, liberal programming. Here's the bureaucratic language in the FCC's job description of the "diversity officer" that would authorize this:

> ...to collect relevant data and assess the interaction between communications service providers and consumers in minority communities and to help develop policies aimed at ensuring that all consumers have the information and service assistance they need to make informed consumer choices.[148]

3) **"Require commercial owners who fail to abide by enforceable public interest obligations to pay a fee to support public broadcasting"** (p. 11). Even though National Public Radio's 860 stations are partially tax-supported and claim a total weekly audience of 26 million, the report says some private sector stations would have to pay for — more public radio. Here's how it would work:

> A fee based on a sliding scale (1 percent for small markets, 5 percent for the largest markets) would be distributed directly to the Corporation for Public Broadcasting with clear mandates to support local news and public affairs programming and to cover controversial and political issues in a fair and balanced manner. We estimate that such a fee would net between $100 million and $250 million and would not overly burden commercial radio broadcasters (p. 11).

And who would determine what is "fair and balanced?" Up till now, the market has spoken, with radio listeners favoring conservative viewpoints. If Mr. Lloyd has his way, this will change, putting government-appointed community organizers instead of consumers in the driver's seat and forcing conservative talk show hosts off the air.

His criteria for replacing current radio management and talent will consist of social engineering and reverse racism. At a 2005 conference, he said:

> There's nothing more difficult than this. Because we have really, truly good white people in important positions. And the fact of the matter is that there are a limited number of those positions. And unless we are conscious of the need to have more people of color, gays, other people in those positions, we will not change the problem. We're in a position where you have to say who is going to step down so someone else can have power.[149]

CHAPTER 8

KEVIN JENNINGS
"SAFE SCHOOLS CZAR"

This might be the most shocking Obama appointment of all. Kevin Jennings, 46, is the founder of the Gay, Lesbian and Straight Education Network (GLSEN), which promotes homosexuality in the nation's schools. On May 19, 2009, he was appointed as the nation's "safe schools czar."

As the Assistant Deputy Secretary for the Office of Safe and Drug Free Schools in the Department of Education, he oversees a $100 million budget and distributes grants to organizations and programs that promote health and prevent violence.[150] This includes "anti-bullying" programs that often promote acceptance of homosexuality.

On its website, GLSEN offers books to children that present a false picture of homosexuality as in-born, natural, and harmless. Many of the books, such as *Rainbow Boys,* include seductions of teens by adults and descriptions of homosexual acts. GLSEN recommends *Rainbow Boys* for grades 7-12.[151]

EXPLICIT READING LIST

As *The Washington Times* reports, "Eleven of the recommended books were examined by Scott Baker from Breitbart.tv.... Numerous passages discuss kids having sex with adults. Many ... are too explicit for us to publish...."[152]

An analysis of the books at Gateway Pundit blog says, "Book after book after book contained stories and anecdotes that weren't merely X-rated and pornographic, but which featured explicit descriptions of sex acts between preschoolers...."[153]

GLSEN co-sponsored a seminar at Tufts University in Massachusetts on March 25, 2000, in which teens as young as 12 were taught specific homosexual sex acts, some of which are patently dangerous. When a parent, Scott Whiteman, revealed audio tapes of the seminar, homosexual activist lawyers tried to get a court to ban distribution of the tape and then sued Whiteman and Brian Camenker, director of the Parents Rights Coalition, which had distributed the tape.[154] Jennings, who was the keynote speaker at what *Massachusetts News* publisher Ed Pawlick later dubbed "Fistgate," was totally unrepentant about kids being exposed to the graphic information and later defended the event.

Jennings, who was a member of the radical homosexual group Act-Up, which disrupted church services and used terror tactics against policymakers and pharmaceutical companies, is listed as a sponsor of an art exhibit at Harvard University entitled "ACT-UP New York: Activism, Art and the AIDS Crisis, 1987-1993," which ran October 15 through December 23, 2009. The exhibit includes a photo of Catholic Cardinal John O'Connor of New York, with large block letters proclaiming "KNOW YOUR SCUMBAGS."[155] O'Connor, who Act-Up activists spat upon during a parade and denounced as a "hater," had quietly opened the city's largest number of AIDS clinics and hospices and made many personal visits to the dying. His compassion work earned him no credit with homosexual activists, only a steady stream of hate-filled expletives.

At a 1997 GLSEN conference, Jennings outlined his goals:

> I'd like five years from now for most Americans, when they hear the word GLSEN, to think, "Ooh, that's good for kids."...

Sane people keep the world the same [sh---y] old way it is now. It's the [crazy] people who think, "No, I can envision a day when straight people say, 'So what if you're promoting homosexuality?' or [when] straight kids say, 'Hey, why don't you and your boyfriend come over before you go to the prom and try your tuxes on at my house?'"... [I]f we believe that can happen, we can make it happen. The only thing that will stop us is our lack of faith that we can make it happen. That is our mission from this day forward.[156]

At the same conference, he said:

One of the people that's always inspired me is Harry Hay, who started the first ongoing gay rights groups in America.

But Hay is more than a gay rights pioneer. He was an outspoken supporter of the North American Man-Boy Love Association (NAMBLA), which promotes sex between men and boys. NAMBLA's slogan is: "Sex before eight, or it's too late." During the 1990s, Hay lobbied for the group's inclusion in "gay pride" parades.

David Thorstad, a self-avowed pedophile who authored articles for *Paedika, the Journal of Paedophila,* wrote this about Harry Hay on NAMBLA's website:

Harry was a vocal and courageous supporter of NAMBLA and intergenerational sexual relationships.... I was introduced to him ... by lesbian activist, self-professed witch, and sometime weed partner Katherine Davenport, a mutual friend and journalist for the *New York Native.* I knew about Harry's past as a Communist and labor activist...."[157]

Under Jennings, GLSEN initiated gay/straight alliances in public schools and events such as the disruptive "Day of Silence," "No Name-Calling Week" and "Ally Week," when, under the guise of discouraging bullying, kids are taught to promote homosexuality and accuse anyone who thinks it is immoral of being a bigot and hater.

Jennings is also credited as the author of a questionnaire distributed in Massachusetts schools that encourages kids to question their sexuality.

As WorldNetDaily.com reports:

> MassResistance.com, a pro-family group in Massachusetts, has identified Jennings as the author of the "Heterosexism questionnaire" that has appeared in schools.
>
> In his book, *Becoming Visible*, the organization notes, the following questions appear under Jennings' book byline and without any other attribution:
>
> 1. What do you think caused your heterosexuality?
> 2. When and how did you first decide you were heterosexual?
> 3. Is it possible heterosexuality is a phase you will grow out of?
> 4. Is it possible you are heterosexual because you fear the same sex?
> 5. If you have never slept with someone of the same sex, how do you know you wouldn't prefer that? Is it possible you merely need a good gay experience?
> 6. To whom have you disclosed your heterosexuality? How did they react?
> 7. Heterosexuality isn't offensive as long as you leave others alone. Why, however, do so many heterosexuals try to seduce others into their orientation?
> 8. Most child molesters are heterosexual. Do you consider it safe to expose your children

to heterosexuals? Heterosexual teachers particularly?

9. Why are heterosexuals so blatant, always making a spectacle of their heterosexuality? Why can't they just be who they are and not flaunt their sexuality by kissing in public, wearing wedding rings, etc.?

10. How can you have a truly satisfying relationship with someone of the opposite sex, given the obvious physical and emotional differences?

11. Heterosexual marriage has total societal support, yet over half of all heterosexuals who marry this year will divorce. Why are there so few successful heterosexual relationships?

12. Given the problems heterosexuals face, would you want your children to be heterosexual? Would you consider aversion therapy to try to change them?

"They're just flipping reality on its head, denying there even is a normal," said [MassResistance] spokeswoman Amy Contrada.

JENNINGS TO CHRISTIANS: "DROP DEAD"

At a March 20, 2000, conference at a church, Jennings called Moral Majority and Liberty University founder Jerry Falwell a terrorist, and said:

We have to quit being afraid of the religious right. We also have to quit — ... I'm trying to find a way to say this. I'm trying not to say, '[F---] 'em!' which is what I want to say, because I don't care what they think! [audience laughter] Drop dead![158]

Ironically, GLSEN's annual conferences are called "Teaching

Respect for All."

As a schoolteacher in Concord, Massachusetts, Jennings covered up a sexual incident between a teen boy and a man at a bus station restroom. Here is a description from a September 28, 2009, *Washington Times* editorial:

> According to Mr. Jennings' own description in a new audiotape discovered by Fox News, the 15-year-old boy met the "older man" in a "bus station bathroom" and was taken to the older man's home that night. When some details about the case became public, Mr. Jennings threatened to sue another teacher who called his failure to report the statutory rape "unethical." Mr. Jennings' defenders asserted that there was no evidence that he was aware the student had sex with the older man.
>
> However, the new audiotape contradicts this claim. In 2000, Mr. Jennings gave a talk to the Iowa chapter of the Gay, Lesbian and Straight Education Network, an advocacy group that promotes homosexuality in schools. On the tape, Mr. Jennings recollected that he told the student to make sure "to use a condom" when he was with the older man. That he actively encouraged the relationship is reinforced by Mr. Jennings' own description in his 1994 book, *One Teacher in 10*. In that account, the teacher boasts how he allayed the student's concerns about the relationship to such a degree that the 15-year-old "left my office with a smile on his face that I would see every time I saw him on the campus for the next two years, until he graduated."[159]

Jennings wrote the foreword to the 1999 book *Queering Elementary Education: Advancing the Dialogue about Sexualities and Schooling.* Among its essays is one featuring an eight-year-old girl named Steph, who "attends queer events with her parents' friends," is taught about masturbation, and whose mom is attracted to the same 12-year-old girl as Steph.[160] On the back cover of the book, which rails against "heteronormative" culture, is a tribute from William Ayers, the friend of Barack Obama who was a domestic terrorist with the Weather Underground and served with Obama at two foundations in Chicago.

Kevin Jennings
Newscom

"SAFE SEX" GUIDE

In 2005, GLSEN distributed a "safe sex" guide to Massachusetts high schoolers that included the addresses and phone numbers of homosexual bars. As *The Washington Times* notes in an editorial:

> The guide's descriptions of what goes on in these bars is explicit. Over here, there's "dancing, young guys and those who like young guys." Over there, the ambience is "old school, cruisy, sex-charged late at night." At another hot spot, there's "porn on the television, the old, the young. Something for everyone."
>
> ...Jennings defenders accuse anyone who dares question this senior presidential appointee with hate and homophobia. That's a twisted moral universe where protecting homosexual minors from predators is "hate," while helping teens become conveniently alcohol-addled prey is, what ... love?[161]

The *Times* is actually being quite cautious. The booklet in question has a lot more than gay bars in it. And the item on the bar with "porn on the television" is for the club Paradise, and begins: "Strippers dancing on the pool tables and bonking their heads on the overhead lights."[162]

On April 30, 2005, a year after Gov. Mitt Romney ordered the issuance of marriage licenses for same-sex couples, GLSEN sponsored a statewide series of conferences in Massachusetts for students and teachers. At Brookline High School, the booklet referenced above, entitled *Little Black Book*, and authored with support from the Massachusetts Department of Public Health and several publically funded Boston-based health and AIDS organizations, was handed out. The booklet is so explicit and shocking that much of its contents cannot be quoted here. Complete with pornographic photos and obscene language, the book instructs kids in how to perform various sex acts with the rectum, including oral sex, urinating on each other, and more. For those understandably repelled by even this brief description, keep in mind that far more explicit material is being given to youngsters.

Little Black Book includes "Your Sexual Rights & Responsibilities" and lists three:

- You have the right to enjoy sex without shame or stigma.
- You have the right to safer sex materials that speak to your desires.
- You have the right to take action for your community! Be heard, you are the expert.[163]

Do you hear that message? They are telling kids that they have a "right" to any behavior imaginable, no matter how dangerous, couching it in "safe" terms, and even urging them to become activists to promote it to others. Satan himself could not have fashioned a more alluring message for sexually confused kids looking to justify forays into perverse, unhealthy sex. And the man whose organization is promoting the campaign to corrupt kids nationwide is the nation's "safe schools czar," or at least was at the time of this writing.

On October 15, 2009, more than 50 congressmen signed a letter to President Obama relating Jennings' radical background and asking that he be replaced. The letter notes Jennings' long history of promoting "the homosexual agenda in schools," and that in his 2006 memoir, *Mama's Boy, Preacher's Son,* "Mr. Jennings describes his use of illegal drugs without expressing regret or acknowledging the devastating effects illegal drug use can have on a person's life."

"Given these very serious issues with Mr. Jennings' record, we urge you to remove him immediately."

Nearly 2,000 years ago, gathering children around him, Jesus Christ issued this warning:

> Whoever causes one of these little ones who believe in Me to sin, it would be better for him if a millstone were hung around his neck, and he were drowned in the depth of the sea (Matthew 18:6).

And the Apostle Paul warned in the Book of Romans that when people cease honoring God and His Word, it will go badly for them:

> ... although they knew God, they did not glorify Him as God, nor were thankful, but became futile in their thoughts, and their foolish hearts were darkened. Professing to be wise, they became fools.... Therefore God also gave them up to uncleanness, in the lusts of their hearts, to dishonor their bodies among themselves..." (Romans 1:21, 22, 24).
>
> For this reason God gave them up to vile passions. For even their women exchanged the natural use for what is against nature. Likewise also the men, leaving the natural use of the woman, burned in their lust for one another, men with men committing what is shameful, and receiving in themselves the penalty of their error which was due (Romans 1:26, 27).

But Paul also gave all sinners, including those tempted by homosexual sin, hope for change:

> And such were some of you. But you were washed, but you were sanctified, but you were justified in the name of the Lord Jesus and by the Spirit of our God (I Corinthians 6:11).

CHAPTER 9

JOHN HOLDREN
"SCIENCE CZAR"

"It is time we once again put science at the top of our agenda and worked to restore America's place as the world leader in science and technology.... Because the truth is that promoting science isn't just about providing resources — it's about protecting free and open inquiry. It's about ensuring that facts and evidence are never twisted or obscured by politics or ideology."

—President-elect Barack Obama, announcing the appointment of John Holdren as "science czar" on December 20, 2008.[164]

One of the earliest Obama appointments, John Holdren as "science czar," signaled the Obama Administration's intention to harness "science" to a radical social agenda, despite Obama's stated intentions. Director of the White House's Office of Science and Technology Policy and Co-Chair of the President's Council of Advisors on Science and Technology, Holdren has a broad mandate to advise the president on all matters scientific, including space exploration, environmental policies, health initiatives, and more.[165]

RADICAL CAREER

Holdren, 65, has a far-left worldview, beginning with his emergence as a "radical scientist" warning of overpopulation in the 1960s and 1970s, and continuing with doomsday warnings of catastrophic global warming up to this day.

Director of the science policy program at Harvard's Kennedy School of Government for the past 13 years, until his presidential appointment on December 20, 2008, Dr. Holdren has a long track record of espousing radical positions, such as establishing a "planetary regime" of global government that could order mandatory abortions and compulsory sterilization, including spiking water supplies with a birth control chemical.

In 1976, he co-authored the book *Ecoscience: Population, Resources, Environment*[166] with Paul and Anne Ehrlich. Paul Ehrlich is best known for his 1968 book *The Population Bomb*, in which he wrongly predicted worldwide famines killing "hundreds of millions" beginning in the 1970s.

In *Ecoscience,* Holdren and the Ehrlichs summarize their "planetary regime" view: "To provide a high quality of life for all, there must be fewer people," hence they floated some population control measures. Since Holdren's appointment, he and the Ehrlichs have said that they do not believe in such coercive policies and that these were merely ideas that they wrote about in their '70s book that have been taken out of context.

You can judge for yourself by reading some passages in which the authors embrace the now-discredited, extremely pessimistic view propounded in 1798 by Thomas Malthus.

Holdren and the Ehrlichs, as quoted below by Ben Johnson in Frontpagemag.com, did not see the United States Constitution as a bar to forced abortions:

> "... [I]t has been concluded that compulsory population-control laws, even including laws requiring *compulsory abortion, could be sustained under the existing constitution,* if the population crisis became sufficiently

severe to endanger the society" (emphasis added). To underscore they mean business, they conclude, "If some individuals contribute to general social deterioration by overproducing children, and if the need is compelling, they can be required by law to exercise reproductive responsibility" (pp. 837-838).[167]

Johnson also quotes this self-defining passage from *Ecoscience*: "'The neo-Malthusian view proposes ... population limitation and redistribution of wealth.' They concluded, 'On these points, we find ourselves firmly in the neo-Malthusian camp'" (p. 954).

Also undercutting the idea that the authors were somehow taken out of context is an exchange on February 12, 2009, during Holdren's confirmation hearing in the Senate Committee on Commerce, Science and Transportation between Holdren and Sen. David Vitter (R-La.) concerning Holdren's prior warnings of ecological disaster.

Vitter asked Holdren to explain his 1986 prediction that global warming was going to kill about 1 billion people by 2020.

"You would still say," Vitter asked, "that 1 billion people lost by 2020 is still a possibility?"

Holdren replied: "It is a possibility, and one we should work energetically to avoid."[168]

As one of the most visible and influential scientists in America, Holdren has used his bully pulpit the last few years to advance global warming in forums such as *The New York Times,* where, in a 2008 column, he lamented the existence of a "denier fringe" of "climate change skeptics that infest talk shows, Internet blogs, letters to the editor, op-ed pieces, and cocktail-party conversations." He darkly warns that this discussion should be brought to a close:

> The extent of unfounded skepticism about the disruption
> of global climate by human-produced greenhouse gases
> is not just regrettable, it is dangerous. It has delayed —
> and continues to delay — the development of the political

consensus that will be needed if society is to embrace remedies commensurate with the challenge.[169]

In keeping with his often-stated desire to place the world under a global, environmentally empowered government is his criticism of the United States. In a 2007 speech to the American Association for the Advancement of Science, which he served as president 2006-2007, he said:

> The United States, by far the richest country in the world in gross national income, is the stingiest among all the OECD (Organization for Economic Cooperation and Development) countries in the fraction of it, 0.2%, devoted to ODA (official development assistance). [Americans spend 3.5 times more on tobacco and 20 times more on defense.][170]

Like most socialists, Holdren ignores the enormous charitable giving from America's private sector, seeing only government as a factor. He also neglects to mention that other nations have more money to spare for social purposes if America is bearing the brunt of military spending to keep the world free.

In a footnote, he makes this observation:

> The United States compounds its distinction as the meanest of wealthy countries in aid-giving by claiming the record for the fraction of its aid that is 'tied': that is, the money must be used to purchase goods and services from the donor.[171]

He might have a point, except that this is one way to curb the tendency of Third World kleptocrats from socking it away in their Swiss bank accounts or in gambling trips to Monaco.

Before the global warming theory took hold as the Left's preferred way to obtain ultimate power and world governance, many scientists – as well as journalists – used to believe that the earth was too cool, not becoming too hot. The media's schizophrenic coverage is well documented in the Special Report "Fire and Ice" from the Media Research Center.[172] For example, the March 1, 1975, *Science News* magazine cover featured a drawing of a city being overwhelmed with glacial ice and the headline, "The Ice Age Cometh?"[173]

John Holdren
Newscom

Time magazine warned on June 24, 1974, that "climatological Cassandras are becoming increasingly apprehensive that weather aberrations they are studying may be the harbinger of a new ice age."[174] On May 21, 1975, *The New York Times* ran a story, "Scientists Ponder Why World's Climate Is Changing: A Major Cooling Widely Considered to Be Inevitable."[175]

HOLDREN'S HERO

Holdren's role model, geochemist Harrison Brown, wrote a 1954 book, *The Challenge of Man's Future*, that even suggested that carbon dioxide be pumped into the atmosphere to create a greenhouse effect to create longer growing seasons.[176]

WorldNetDaily's Jerome Corsi quotes Brown:

"If, in some manner, the carbon-dioxide content of the atmosphere could be increased threefold, world food production might be doubled."

Brown was clear that world governments should cooperate to generate excess carbon dioxide, not to reduce human-generated carbon dioxide from the atmosphere.

"One can visualize, on a world scale, huge carbon-dioxide generators pouring the gas into the atmosphere," he wrote.[177]

Corsi documents Holdren's admiration for Brown, who was a member of the International Eugenics Society:

> In 1986, science czar Holdren co-edited a scientific reader, "Earth and the Human Future: Essays in Honor of Harrison Brown."
>
> In one of his introductory essays written for the book, Holdren acknowledged he read Brown's *The Challenge of Man's Future* when he was in high school and that the book had a profound effect on his intellectual development.
>
> Holdren acknowledged Brown's book transformed his thinking about the world and "about the sort of career I wanted to pursue."
>
> Holdren further commented in glowing terms that Brown's book was a work "that should have reshaped permanently the perceptions of all serious analysts about the interactions of the demographic, biological, geophysical, technological, economic and sociopolitical dimensions of contemporary problems."[178]

Among other observations in Harrison Brown's book was the need for an all-powerful government in which the "number of abortions and artificial inseminations permitted in a given year would be determined completely by the difference between the number of deaths and the number of births in the year previous."[179]

This kind of totalitarian impulse is mirrored in Holdren's own writing, with the Ehrlichs in 1977 in which they prescribed:

> ...organized evasive action: population control, limitation of material consumption, redistribution of wealth, transitions to technologies that are environmentally and socially less disruptive than today's, and *movement toward some kind of world government*[180] (emphasis added).

The White House and Holdren have said that Holdren is not as radical as his earlier writings indicate, and suggested that critics read more recent works. Here's columnist Michelle Malkin's response:

> Well, I did read one of Holdren's recent works. It revealed his clingy reverence for, and allegiance to, the gurus of population control authoritarianism. He's just gotten smarter about cloaking it behind global warming hysteria. In 2007, he addressed the American Association for the Advancement of Science conference. Holdren served as AAAS president; the organization posted his full slide presentation on its website.
>
> In the opening slide, Holdren admitted that his "preoccupation" with apocalyptic matters such as "the rates at which people breed" was a lifelong obsession spurred by Harrison Brown's work. Holdren heaped praise on Brown's half-century-old book, *The Challenge of Man's Future*, and then proceeded to paint doom-and-gloom scenarios requiring drastic government interventions to control climate change.[181]

If there is any doubt where Holdren wants to take science and public policy, President Obama gave a clear indication in his first few weeks in office, when he signed an executive order lifting the ban on federally funded embryonic stem cell research, overturning the "Mexico City" policy that barred U.S. tax dollars going to international groups that promote or perform abortions; restored U.S. funding to the United Nations pro-abortion Population Fund, and ordered a review of "conscience" laws that protect doctors and hospitals from being forced to perform abortions or distribute contraceptives.[182] The actions had "population control" written all over them.

Holdren's name also appeared frequently in the "Climategate" e-mails that surfaced in November 2009 from the Climatic Research Unit (CRU) at the University of East Anglia in Great Britain, which is a chief source of data for the United Nations' Intergovernmental Panel on Climate Change (IPCC).[183] The IPCC is the driving force behind the effort to create world government via the climate change scare. The cache of thousands of emails reveals that scientists destroyed raw temperature data that conflicted with global warming theory and discussed ways to discredit dissenting scientists and even scientific journals that dared to question the man-made theory of global warming. The IPCC was a co-recipient with Al Gore of the 2007 Nobel Peace Prize "for their efforts to build up and disseminate greater knowledge about man-made climate change, and to lay the foundations for the measures that are needed to counteract such change."[184]

As the Essex County Conservative Examiner summarizes:

> Holdren was directly complicit in impugning the credibility of certain physicists who challenged the orthodox opinion on anthropogenic global warming (AGW), specifically with reference to the Medieval Warm Period of 800-1300, that preceded the Little Ice Age of 1400-1850. These physicists, Sallie Baliunas and Willie Soon, published a paper in 2003, "Proxy climatic and environmental changes of the past 1000 years," in the journal *Climate Research*, explaining their findings. In brief, they correlated average temperature, using humidity as a proxy, with sunspot activity, and found that sunspot activity correlated well with the Medieval Warm Period and the Little Ice Age.[185]

While Holdren and other true believers in apocalyptic global warming continue to try to consolidate government power over more and more human activity, the number of dissenting scientists keeps growing. A petition signed by 31,478 scientists states:

> There is no convincing scientific evidence that human release of carbon dioxide, methane, or other greenhouse gases is causing or will, in the foreseeable future, cause catastrophic heating of the Earth's atmosphere and disruption of the Earth's climate. Moreover, there is substantial scientific evidence that increases in

atmospheric carbon dioxide produce many beneficial effects upon the natural plant and animal environments of the Earth.[186]

ENVIRONMENTAL RADICALS: THE EARLY YEARS.

The term "Malthusian" comes from British political economist Thomas Robert Malthus, whose gloomy view that population growth would outstrip resources led him to write a famous essay in 1798 advocating measures to limit the number of people. Here's a startling excerpt from his *Essay on the Principle of Population*:

> All the children born, beyond what would be required to keep up the population to this level, must necessarily perish, unless room be made for them by the deaths of grown persons....
>
> To act consistently therefore, we should facilitate, instead of foolishly and vainly endeavouring to impede, the operations of nature in producing this mortality; and if we dread the too frequent visitation of the horrid form of famine, we should sedulously encourage the other forms of destruction, which we compel nature to use.
>
> Instead of recommending cleanliness to the poor, we should encourage contrary habits. In our towns we should make the streets narrower, crowd more people into the houses, **and court the return of the plague.** In the country, we should build our villages near stagnant pools,

and particularly encourage settlements in all marshy and unwholesome situations. But above all, we should reprobate [disallow or reject] specific remedies for ravaging diseases; and those benevolent, but much mistaken men, who have thought they were doing a service to mankind by projecting schemes for the total extirpation of particular disorders[187] (emphasis added).

CHAPTER 10

CAROL BROWNER
"CLIMATE CHANGE CZARINA"

The "Climate Change Czarina" is a driving force behind the proposed "cap and trade" bill (Waxman-Markey) that would create a massive federal bureaucracy to curb carbon emissions, shackle businesses with onerous regulations, and impose the largest tax increase in American history.

She is also a Socialist (yes, capital S) and a former board director of APX, Inc., a firm that facilitates trading of billions of dollars of carbon offsets that would be required by the proposed law. Here is APX's own description from its website:

> APX is policy-neutral; it does not take positions in the markets, and its revenues are unrelated to the market prices for the environmental and cap-and-trade market certificates its systems create, track, manage and retire. APX is the system of choice for every major renewable energy market in North America and greenhouse gas

markets worldwide.... Providing a bank and mint for environmental commodities...."[188]

Browner, 54, was also on the board of the radical Center for American Progress, a left-wing think tank funded by billionaire George Soros.[189]

Carol Browner
Zuma/Michael Quan

Browner directed the Environmental Protection Agency for most of the Clinton Administration, during which President Clinton attempted unsuccessfully to elevate the position to the level of a cabinet secretary. She is considered a protégé of former Vice President Al Gore, and served as his Legislative Director toward the end of his U.S. Senate career, from 1988 to 1991.

In 2007, she married former New York Democratic Congressman Thomas Downey, who served a Long Island district from 1975 to 1993. Browner and Downey worked together in 2006 lobbying Congress for approval for the Dubai Ports World deal, which would have transferred management of six major U.S. shipping ports to DP World, a corporation wholly owned by the United Arab Emirates.

MEMBER OF SOCIALIST INTERNATIONAL

Browner was a member of the Commission for a Sustainable World Society (CSWS), an elite arm of an anti-capitalist and frequently anti-America group called the Socialist International.[190] As such, she may be formally described as a Socialist. The Socialist International, whose slogan is "Progressive Politics *for a fairer world*" (italics in original), is "the worldwide organisation of social democratic, socialist and labour parties."[191] This fact was discovered by the *Washington Examiner* during her confirmation hearings in early 2009, at which point her membership and photograph were scrubbed from the CSWS's website. A list of speakers for their 2008 Athens conference still describes her as a member of the organization.[192]

The *Examiner* observed in an editorial:

The Socialist International is no group of woolly-headed idealists. It is an influential assembly of officials from across the international community whose official Statement of Principles describes an agenda of gaining and exercising government power based on socialist concepts.... By appointing Browner to a White House post, Obama has at the least implicitly endorsed an utterly radical socialist agenda for his administration's environmental policy. The incoming chief executive thus strengthens critics who contend environmental policies aren't really about protecting endangered species or preserving virgin lands, but rather expanding government power and limiting individual freedom.[193]

According to Fox News, President Obama

has said that taking action on climate change will be a priority in his administration. An Obama spokesman

Screenshot from Socialist International website shows Carol Browner speaking at the Socialist International Congress in Greece in 2008.

said Browner's membership in Socialist International is not a problem, and that she brings "indispensable" experience in policymaking to her new role as Obama's top environmental adviser, a position that does not require Senate confirmation.[194]

As Director of the White House Office of Energy and Climate Change Policy, Browner could be considered more powerful than some cabinet secretaries, since she wields authority over matters that involve the Environmental Protection Agency, the Energy Department and the Department of the Interior. President Obama said she will "create jobs, achieve energy security, and combat climate change."[195]

"She is pretty extremist in my eyes in terms of her liberal leanings," Sen. Jim Inhofe (R-OK) told reporters. "Where do you draw the line between an extreme liberal and a Socialist? You know, everyone has a different view of that."[196]

SECRET TALKS WITH AUTO EXECS

She also may not believe in the vaunted "transparency" that President Obama pledged to bring to his administration. After President Obama imposed tough new emissions standards on the auto industry on May 19, 2009, the *Washington Examiner* reported that Browner had led secret talks on the Corporate Average Fuel Economy (CAFÉ) standards and warned auto industry executives "to put nothing in writing — ever."[197] *The Examiner* reported that

> Rep. James Sensenbrenner (R-WI) is demanding a congressional investigation of Browner's conduct in the CAFE talks, saying in a letter to Rep. Henry Waxman (D-CA) that Browner "intended to leave little or no documentation of the deliberations that led to stringent new CAFE standards."
>
> Federal law requires officials to preserve documents concerning significant policy decisions, so instructing participants in a policy negotiation concerning a major

federal policy change could be viewed as a criminal act.

As the administration's point person on global warming, Browner helped push through the House version of the 1,000-plus page Cap and Trade bill (Waxman-Markey) in June 2009, which passed without most members of Congress reading it. A week later, on June 29, Browner appeared on Fox News Channel and was befuddled when asked whether she herself had read the bill. When pressed, she finally said she "had read vast portions of it."[198]

In November 2009, thousands of e-mails from scientists at the Climate Research Unit at the University of East Anglia (UEA) in Great Britain were released, exposing researchers' deliberate destruction of inconvenient temperature data, attempts to blacklist scientists critical of the global warming theory, and threats to undermine the credibility of journals that publish contrary information. The revelations have enormous significance, because the CRU is a major source of data for the Intergovernmental Panel on Climate Change,[199] the group created by the United Nations and the World Meteorological Organization to spearhead international carbon reduction efforts and the rise of a global government.

When a researcher collecting data for this book contacted the White House in order to get Browner's opinion on "Climategate" the White House staff referred all calls to their press office, which claimed no knowledge of the e-mails more than a week after the story broke. However, on November 25, 2009, *The Washington Times* reported that Browner had, indeed weighed in on the controversy, dismissing concerns and saying that the issue had been settled.

She derided critics of manmade global warming (which include 31,000 scientists who have signed a petition) as "a very small group of people who say this isn't a real problem."[200]

CHAPTER 11

CASS SUNSTEIN
"REGULATORY CZAR"

ass Sunstein, the former University of Chicago and Harvard Law professor, is informally called the "regulatory czar." As Administrator of the Office of Information and Regulatory Affairs, he is a de facto "bureaucrat-in-chief," and has advanced so many radical ideas that it's hard to decide where to begin.

But let's start with his advocacy of extreme animal rights. In a 2004 book *Animal Rights: Current Debates and New Directions*, which he co-wrote with then-girlfriend left-wing University of Chicago Law professor Martha Nussbaum, Sunstein, 55, made the case that dogs and cats, not to mention cows and pigs, should have the right to sue people.

> [A]nimals should be permitted to bring suit, with human beings as their representatives, to prevent violations of current law.... Any animals that are entitled to bring suit would be represented by (human) counsel, who would owe

guardian like obligations and make decisions, subject to those obligations, on their clients' behalf.[201]

To establish such a right, a law would have to be enacted.

Animals lack standing as such, simply because no relevant statute confers a cause of action on animals. It seems possible, however, that before long, Congress will grant standing to animals to protect their own rights and interests.[202]

Okay, we have to ask: Is he talking about Congress or animals? If the implications were not so serious, this could be funny.

As Scott Wheeler and Peter Leitner observe in *Shadow Government*:

In a much more sinister development, however, such a legislation would open the floodgates to frivolous lawsuits by environmental and government activists on behalf of wildlife, against any energy or manufacturing company that consumes natural resources and produces waste materials — which pretty much describes all of them. Such a backdoor way to harness intractable businesses is likely to be the real reason why this plan was hatched in the first place.[203]

At an April 2007 Harvard conference, Facing Animals, Sunstein also likened the fight for "nonhuman animal" rights to ending human genocide and slavery:

[Humans'] willingness to subject animals to unjustified suffering will be seen ... as a form of unconscionable barbarity ... morally akin to slavery and the mass extermination of human beings.[204]

He also called for an end to using animals in cosmetic testing and greyhound racing, and urged legislation to end hunting:

> We ought to ban hunting, I suggest, if there isn't a purpose other than sport and fun. That should be against the law. It's time now.[205]

Cass Sunstein
Matthew W. Hutchins

Elsewhere in this remarkably revealing presentation, Sunstein said that humans should consider conferring legal "autonomy" and "freedom of choice" on animals. He conceded, citing Princeton ethicist Peter Singer, that eating meat might still be "okay" only if the animal has had a "long and decent life" first,[206] but encouraged people to become vegetarians.[207]

GET RID OF MARRIAGE

Matching his radical proposals for animal rights, Sunstein is just as adamant about overturning millennia of God-created human institutions, particularly marriage.

In a 2008 book, *Nudge: Improving Decisions About Health, Wealth and Happiness*, Sunstein and his co-author Richard Thaler wrote:

> Under our proposal, the word marriage would no longer appear in any laws, and marriage licenses would no longer be offered or recognized by any level of government.... The only legal status states would confer on couples would be a civil union, which would be a domestic partnership agreement between any two people.[208]

Sunstein and Thaler say that marriage imposes "serious economic and material disadvantages" on single people, so:

Why not leave people's relationships to their own choices, subject to the judgments of private organizations, religious and otherwise?[209]

Sunstein and Thaler also support "routine removal" of human organs because:

[T]he state owns the rights to body parts of people who are dead or in certain hopeless conditions, and it can remove their organs without asking anyone's permission. Though it may sound grotesque, routine removal is not impossible to defend. In theory, it would save lives, and it would do so without intruding on anyone who has any prospect for life.[210]

The authors acknowledge that not everybody might think this is a good idea, so they discuss "presumed consent" as a way to get at the organs:

Although presumed consent is an extremely effective way to increase the supply of organs available for transplant, it may not be an easy sell politically. Some will object to the idea of "presuming" anything when it comes to such a sensitive matter. We are not sure that these objections are convincing, but this is surely a domain in which forced choosing, or what is referred to in this domain as mandated choice, has considerable appeal.[211]

In other words, they want an opt-out program in which the state assumes it can take your organs unless you say otherwise.

Sunstein also thinks the government should pay for abortion, since government pays for some women's childbirth expenses. WorldNetDaily's Aaron Klein quotes Sunstein as follows from Sunstein's 1991 book, *The Partial Constitution*:

"I have argued that the Constitution ... forbids government from refusing to pay the expenses of abortion in cases of rape or incest, at least if government pays for childbirth in such cases."

In the book, obtained and reviewed by WND, Sunstein sets forth a radical new interpretation of the Constitution. The book contains a chapter entitled "It's the government's money," in which Sunstein strongly argues the government should be compelled to fund abortions for women victimized by rape or incest. The Obama czar posits that funding only childbirth but not abortion "has the precise consequence of turning women into involuntary incubators."[212]

REGULATE FREE SPEECH

The most consistent aspect of Sunstein's paper trail of legal writing is that he supports policies and laws that empower the government and disempower individuals. For instance, Sunstein is one of the most outspoken supporters of a return to the Fairness Doctrine for radio broadcasting, which had throttled on-air discussion of issues until the FCC did away with it in 1987.

Sunstein, however, wants to go even beyond the Fairness Doctrine and have the federal government regulate the Internet, particularly independent bloggers. In 1995, in his book, *Democracy and the Problem of Free Speech*, he proposed a "New Deal for Speech," and said this:

A legislative effort to regulate broadcasting in the interest of democratic principles should not be seen as an abridgment of the free speech guarantee.[213]

In the 2007 book, *Republic.com 2.0*, he says:

A system of limitless individual choices, with respect to communications, is not necessarily in the interest of citizenship and self-government.[214]

In 2008, Sunstein pulled back a bit, saying at a UCLA Law School debate that, "I don't want government regulation of the blogosphere in the form of mandated links or mandated civility or, you know, if you're doing liberal ideas on your site you have to have conservative ideas too."[215] Instead, he said, bloggers should employ "private, voluntary solutions"[216] which is a departure from many earlier exhortations toward more government control. It will be interesting to see where he comes down on "net neutrality," a debate about Internet regulation that will heat up in 2010.

DISDAIN FOR GUN RIGHTS

Another prime example of Sunstein's reflexive search for government solutions is his disdain for the Second Amendment's guarantee of the right to bear arms.

In his book *Radicals in Robes*, Sunstein argues that Americans have no such individual right:

> [A]lmost all gun control legislation is constitutionally fine. And if the Court is right then fundamentalism does not justify the view that the Second Amendment protects an individual right to bear arms.[217]

Sunstein also wrote:

> Consider the view that the Second Amendment confers an individual right to own guns. The view is respectable, but it may be wrong, and prominent specialists reject it on various grounds. As late as 1980, it would have been preposterous to argue that the Second Amendment creates an individual right to own guns, and no federal court invalidated a gun control restriction on Second Amendment grounds until 2007.[218]

Sunstein went on to blame the National Rifle Association and other "energetic" pro-gun "entrepreneurs." That group might have to be expanded to include the United States Supreme Court, which upheld individual gun rights in federal enclaves in the *District of Columbia v. Heller* case in 2008. Sunstein characterized that ruling as being based less on the Constitution than on the influence of the gun lobby on public attitudes:

> In the context of use of guns, it might be helpful to emphasize that the National Rifle Association is funded in large part by gun manufacturers, and that manufacturers of guns are often behind efforts to claim that the Constitution guarantees rights of gun ownership.[219]

In his long advocacy of abortion rights, Sunstein may have made similar comments about Planned Parenthood, NARAL Pro-Choice America, and other players in the abortion lobby and their effect on legal rulings and public polling, but I have not run across any.

In the *Heller* case, Sunstein basically accuses the Court of being in the grip of popular opinion:

> The Supreme Court's ruling in favor of an individual's right to bear arms for military purposes was not really a statement on behalf of the Constitution, as it was written by those long dead; it was based on judgments that are now widespread among the living.[220]

Another case, *McDonald vs. City of Chicago*, testing Chicago's strict gun law and which may determine whether states and cities have the right to ban guns, was to be heard in early 2010.[221]

True believers in government see the public sector as a panacea for all problems. In his book *The Second Bill of Rights: FDR's Unfinished Revolution and Why We Need It More Than Ever*, Sunstein writes:

> My major aim in this book is to uncover an important but neglected part of America's heritage: the idea of a second bill of rights. In brief, the second bill attempts to protect

both opportunity and security, by creating rights to
employment, adequate food and clothing, decent shelter,
education, recreation, and medical care.[222]

Of course, for the government to guarantee a "right" to all of these
things, the government itself would have to control all aspects of life, and be,
in effect, a communist system.

Given the breadth and depth of the changes that Obama and the radical
leaders of the U.S. Congress are attempting to impose, there is simply no
logical stopping point. They see private ownership and income as things
rightly owned by the government and that any earnings we keep for our own
families are a gift from the government.

In short, they mean to turn Caesar into our God, and the sooner the
better. A "regulatory czar" with leftist tendencies and far-reaching powers fits
nicely into that scheme.

CHAPTER 12

HAROLD KOH
STATE DEPARTMENT
LEGAL ADVISOR

I f anyone epitomizes the Obama Administration's dedication to do away with "American exceptionalism" and appease international elites at the expense of U.S. interests and sovereignty, it is Harold Koh, 55, whom Obama appointed as the top lawyer for the State Department.

Among other things, Koh has long supported closing the Guantanamo Bay detention center and bringing al Qaeda terrorists to the U.S. to be tried in criminal courts. He also favors making state and federal laws conform to "international" standards, and ceding more American sovereignty through treaties. He once referred to President Bush as "the torturer in chief."[223]

Under Koh's leadership, the Yale Law School filed suit against one of its own alumni, John Yoo, for his Justice Department legal memos following the September 11, 2001, attacks concerning the permissible limits of interrogating terror suspects. As *The Wall Street Journal* commented:

Having failed to enact their agenda in Congress, or now

even via Mr. Obama, their aim is to ruin and bankrupt individuals in the Bush Administration who played key roles in the war on terror. Their goal is to make sure that no one in public life ever again offers advice that disagrees with their view that terrorists should be handled in nonmilitary courts like common burglars.[224]

RULE BY INTERNATIONAL LAW

Koh, who was dean of Yale University Law School, is one of the foremost proponents of radical "transnationalism." He was confirmed by the U.S. Senate on June 25, 2009, with five Republicans voting to confirm — Sens. Olympia Snowe (ME), Susan Collins (ME), Richard Lugar (IN), Mel Martinez (FL), and George Voinovich (OH). If Lugar had not earlier provided the sole Republican vote in the Senate Foreign Relations Committee to send the nomination to the floor, Koh's appointment could have been stopped.

Transnationalists believe that national sovereignty is outmoded and that international law should supersede laws enacted by individual countries' legislators — including the United States. The most extreme transnationalists want the international legal system to set norms. Koh is part of that wing. Here is a quotation from a law review article that Koh wrote:

> [D]omestic courts must play a key role in coordinating U.S. domestic constitutional rules with rules of foreign and international law, not simply to promote American aims, but to advance the broader development of a well-functioning international judicial system. In Justice Blackmun's words, U.S. courts must look beyond narrow U.S. interests to the "mutual interests of all nations in a smoothly functioning international legal regime" and, whenever possible, should "consider if there is a course of action that furthers, rather than impedes, the development of an ordered international system."[225]

As chief lawyer for the State Department, Koh is supposed to protect the United States and advance American interests. But his career is full of instances in which he has championed internationalism over American law.

As Hudson Institute foreign policy scholar John Fonte writes,

> Koh's proposed remedy to American exceptionalism is for "American lawyers, scholars and activists" to "trigger a transnational legal process," of "transnational interactions" that will "generate legal interpretations that can in turn be internalized into the domestic law of even resistant nation-states." For example, Koh suggests that "human rights advocates" should litigate "not just in domestic courts, but simultaneously before foreign and international arenas." Moreover, they should encourage foreign governments (such as Mexico) and transnational NGOs to challenge the US on the death penalty and other human rights issues.[226]

Koh has already done enormous damage not only to the rule of law but to America's moral fabric. As the attorney of record in an amicus brief in 2003 in the *Lawrence v. Texas* case in which the U.S. Supreme Court overturned Texas's sodomy law, Koh took the side of internationalist sexual liberals over that of elected Texas state representatives who had enacted the sodomy law on moral, social and public health grounds.

Harold Koh
Newscom

Koh's *Lawrence* brief was filed in the name of the International Human Rights Clinic of Yale University on behalf of Mary Robinson (United Nations High Commissioner for Human Rights from 1997 to 2002 and former president of the Republic of Ireland), Amnesty International, and several other international and domestic "human rights" groups. The brief makes the case that American law should be influenced by international law, and that in some instances, international law is more advanced, humane and progressive than American law and thus should override it. This view conflicts with the oath that U.S. officials take to uphold the Constitution of the United States.

Here's an excerpt from Koh's brief:

> ...Foreign and international courts have barred the criminalization of sodomy between consenting adults.... International and foreign court decisions have triply rejected the understanding of the right to privacy in this Court's decision in *Bowers v. Hardwick*, 478 U.S. 186 (1986).... Finally, international and foreign courts have invalidated same-sex sodomy laws for betraying naked prejudice and a "bare ... desire to harm a politically unpopular group" inconsistent with this Court's equal protection reasoning in *Romer v. Evans*, 517 U.S. 620, 634 (1996) (citation and internal quotation marks omitted). International and foreign rulings demonstrate the irrationality of discriminating against some individuals who commit sodomy, but not others, based solely on their sexual orientation. By their nature, sodomy laws arbitrarily deny persons equal treatment based solely on whom they choose to love.[227]

This argument, which equates disapproval of homosexual sodomy with "naked prejudice" and "irrationality," was quoted approvingly by Justice Anthony Kennedy, who wrote the 5-4 majority opinion in *Lawrence*.

In a scathing dissent, Justice Antonin Scalia warned that the reasoning in *Lawrence* would soon be used as a wrecking ball against marriage laws:

> At the end of its opinion — after having laid waste the

foundations of our rational-basis jurisprudence — the Court says that the present case "does not involve whether the government must give formal recognition to any relationship that homosexual persons seek to enter." *Ante*, at 17. Do not believe it.... Today's opinion dismantles the structure of constitutional law that has permitted a distinction to be made between heterosexual and homosexual unions, insofar as formal recognition in marriage is concerned.[228]

Sure enough, the June 26, 2003, *Lawrence* decision was subsequently cited by the Supreme Judicial Court of Massachusetts, which ruled on November 18, 2003, that Massachusetts' marriage law was unconstitutional. That ruling sparked further court and legislative "gay marriage" activism in California, Connecticut, Iowa, the District of Columbia, New Hampshire, Vermont and Maine. In fact, *Lawrence* is now routinely used as a legal battering ram against any opposition to the radical homosexual political and legal agenda, which is exactly what Koh and his leftist colleagues have long sought.

Perhaps the most chilling aspect of all this is watching legal elites override the moral sensibilities of elected American officials and replacing them with the newly coined prejudices of international elites, which are increasingly anti-Christian, pro-sexual anarchy and anti-democratic. Koh is at the heart of this effort to defeat self-government.

PUSH FOR TREATIES

Koh supports putting the United States under the authority of more and more treaties. In June 2002, he testified before the Senate Foreign Relations committee, urging senators to vote for the United Nations' Convention on the Elimination of All Forms of Discrimination Against Women (CEDAW) treaty, which President Carter had signed in 1980 but the Senate never ratified — for good reason. Here is part of Koh's testimony:

First, ratification would make an important global

statement regarding the seriousness of our national commitment to these issues [of women's human rights]. Second, ratification would have a major impact in ensuring both the appearance and the reality that our national practices fully satisfy or exceed international standards.[229]

CEDAW is a cauldron of radical feminism, homosexuality, and collectivist policies, despite its purported aim to curb violence against women and raise women's status in nations where women are second-class citizens. The CEDAW committee that interprets the treaty has wielded it like a club against traditional mores in many countries, even sinking so low as to attack Mother's Day in Eastern Europe. For some of the most egregious examples, see the Appendix on CEDAW.

There's much, much more, especially in Ed Whelan's excellent series on Koh at *National Review Online*.[230]

But in summary: President Obama has named as America's "lawyer to the world" someone with a profoundly radical, aggressively anti-American agenda.

CHAPTER 13

STEVEN CHU
SECRETARY OF ENERGY

A 1997 Nobel Prize winner for his work with lasers, Dr. Steven Chu is an accomplished scientist. Before his federal agency appointment, he was director of the Lawrence Berkeley National Lab, and professor of Physics and Molecular and Cell Biology at the University of California.[231]

Dr. Chu, 61, is an aggressive backer of the more extreme theories of global warming and has predicted catastrophic outcomes if carbon emissions are not curbed.

In keeping with the liberal-Left's view of Americans as spoiled brats that need government parenting, Chu said,

> The American public ... just like your teenage kids, aren't acting in a way that they should act. The American public has to really understand in their core how important this issue is.[232]

The Energy Department's sister agency, the Environmental Protection Agency, is taking Chu at his word, so don't be surprised if your kids start badgering you about using the new compact fluorescent light (CFL) bulbs instead of the incandescent kind, and trading in your van for a minicar. The EPA in September 2009 announced a program to be implemented in schools nationwide to hector families over their energy consumption.

Kids from BGCA [Boys and Girls Clubs of America] in 60 locations are conducting energy check-ups at homes and in their communities and educating their peers and families about energy efficiency. Through PTO Today [Parent Teacher Organizations Today], EPA is reaching out to 6,000 schools across the country with "Go Green Nights" to help families learn about energy-efficient changes they can make in their homes and schools to save energy and help fight climate change.[233]

GLOBAL WARMING GLOOM

At the Summit of the Americas on April 18, 2009, Chu predicted that if global warming was not curbed, oceans would rise, islands would disappear, and the United States would suffer as well. Here's a report from Fox News:

[Chu stated:] "Lots of area in Florida will go under. New Orleans at three-meter height is in great peril. If you look at, you know, the Bay Area, where I came from, all three airports would be under water. So this is — this is serious stuff. The impacts could be enormous."

Conservative climate change skeptics immediately denounced Chu's assessment of the threat and potential consequences of global warming.

"Secretary Chu still seems to believe that computer model predictions decades or 100 years from now are some sort of 'evidence' of a looming climate catastrophe," said Marc Morano, executive editor of ClimateDepot.

com and former top aide to global warming critic Sen. Jim Inhofe, R-Okla.

"Secretary Chu's assertions on sea level rise and hurricanes are quite simply being proven wrong by the latest climate data. As the Royal Netherlands Meteorological Institute reported in December 12, 2008: There is 'no evidence for accelerated sea-level rise.'"

Steven Chu
Zuma/Xinhua

Morano said hurricane activity levels in both hemispheres of the globe are at 30-year lows and hurricane experts like MIT's Kerry Emanuel and Tom Knutson of the National Oceanic and Atmospheric Administration "are now backing off their previous dire predictions."[234]

Chu has also suggested that people paint their roofs white to repel the sun's energy. At a Nobel Laureate Symposium in London in May 2009, Chu said:

> If you look at all the buildings and if you make the roofs white and if you make the pavement more of a concrete type of colour rather than a black type of colour and if you do that uniformly, that would be the equivalent of ... reducing the carbon emissions due to all the cars in the world by 11 years — just taking them off the road for 11 years.[235]

In September 2008, in an interview with *The Wall Street Journal*, Chu advocated raising federal gasoline taxes so high that Americans would pay as much as Europeans do.[236] At the time he said this, gas was more than $8 a gallon in Europe. Later, on April 23, 2009, in a House Energy and Commerce Committee hearing, under questioning from Rep. Cliff Stearns (R-Fla.), Chu acknowledged that the idea was "silly."[237]

Fortunately, the emergence of Climategate via the leaked e-mails from the University of East Anglia have more scientists seriously questioning the accuracy of computer-simulated global warming scenarios.

As a counter to Dr. Chu's alarmism, here is a commentary from Dr. William Gray, a renowned hurricane forecaster and Emeritus Professor of Atmospheric Science at Colorado State University. The article from which this is excerpted was originally published on December 8, 2009, on Climatedepot.com.

> Rising levels of CO_2 are not near the threat these alarmists have portrayed them to be. There has yet to be an honest and broad scientific debate on the basic science of CO_2's influence on global temperature. The global climate models predicting large amounts of global warming for a doubling of CO_2 are badly flawed. They should never have been used to establish government climate policy.
>
> The last century's global warming of about 1 degree Fahrenheit is not a consequence of human activities. This warming is primarily the result of a multi-century change in the globe's deep ocean circulation. These ocean current changes have led to a small and gradual increase in the globe's temperature. We are coming out of the Little Ice Age and into a generally warmer climate state. This is akin to the warmer global climate of the Medieval Period. We can do nothing but adapt to such long period natural temperature changes.
>
> The recent "Climategate" revelations coming out of the University of East Anglia are but the tip of a giant iceberg of a well-organized international climate warming

conspiracy that has been gathering momentum for the last 25 years. This conspiracy would become much more manifest if all the e-mails of the publically funded climate research groups of the U.S. and of foreign governments were ever made public.

The disastrous economic consequences of restricting CO_2 emissions from the present by as much as 20 percent by 2020 and 80 percent by 2050 (as being proposed in Copenhagen) have yet to be digested by the general public. Such CO_2 output decreases would cause very large increases in our energy costs, a lowering of our standard of living, and do nothing of significance to improve our climate.

The cap-and-trade bill presently before Congress, the likely climate agreements coming out of the Copenhagen Conference, and the EPA's just announced decision to treat CO_2 as a pollutant represents a grave threat to the industrial world's continued economic development.[238]

But if these ill-conceived power grabs are fully exposed in time, we may not have to paint our roofs white and pedal our bikes to work after all.

CHAPTER 14

DAVID OGDEN
DEPUTY ATTORNEY GENERAL

U nder President Obama, it was expected that the porn industry might find a sympathetic ear, given the smut industry's generous support of liberal politicians and groups like the ACLU.

And so it was not too great a surprise that on March 12, the U.S. Senate voted 65 to 28 to confirm porn attorney David Ogden, 56, to be deputy attorney general.

What might have surprised some observers is that 11 senators from the "Party of Family Values" (Republicans Lamar Alexander, Kit Bond, Susan Collins, Lindsey Graham, Judd Gregg, Jon Kyl, Richard Lugar, presidential nominee John McCain, Olympia Snowe, Arlen Specter [who later became a Democrat] and George Voinovich) joined a nearly unanimous Democrat roster (minus Robert Casey of Pennsylvania) in voting yes on Ogden.[239]

Mr. Ogden not only defended child pornography during the Clinton years, but represented hard-core porn producers, plus *Playboy* and *Penthouse*.

Sen. Patrick Leahy, Vermont Democrat, said Mr. Ogden's legal work on behalf of the porn industry was just a "sliver" of his record and, in any case, did not reflect his "personal" views or values. It's doubtful that lawyers working for corporate polluters or pro-life groups would get that kind of pass.

On December 2, 2009, citing differences with Attorney General Eric Holder, Mr. Ogden resigned and returned to private practice.

VICTORY FOR PORNOGRAPHERS

But his initial presence in the Obama Administration was a major victory for pornographers, the abortion industry, and the homosexual movement, among others. It's hard to imagine a more radical appointee in terms of legal social engineering.

Here's more detail on Mr. Ogden's background.

On November 4, 1993, voting 100 to 0, the U.S. Senate passed a nonbinding resolution censuring the Justice Department for refusing to fully defend the conviction of a child pornography recipient. In that case, *Knox v. United States*,[240] Mr. Ogden had filed a friend of the court brief for the American Civil Liberties Union that argued that close-ups of girls' crotches in videos such as "Little Girl Bottoms (Underside)" and "Little Blondes" were not child pornography and thus merited constitutional protection. A Pennsylvania man, Stephen A. Knox, had received videos in the mail that contained footage of pre-teen and teen-age minor girls in compromising poses. The ACLU and

Ogden said that because the children's crotches were not naked, that the footage was constitutionally protected material. But the court disagreed, saying that a federal statute criminalizing child porn did not require nudity but only "lascivious" images, and that the videos met that test.

A week after the Senate vote, President Clinton

David Ogden
Newscom

issued a letter rebuking Attorney General Janet Reno and asking for tougher child pornography enforcement. A few months later, the House added its censure by a vote of 425 to 3.

If this had been an isolated incident that Mr. Ogden now regrets, that would be one thing, but he has a long track record of siding with radical proponents of the sexual revolution.

Brian Burch, president of the Catholic-based public policy group Fidelis, compiled a memo outlining Mr. Ogden's extensive career issuing briefs on behalf of pornographers, abortionists, and homosexual pressure groups, among others.

Here are a few of Mr. Ogden's other activities:

- Opposed the Children's Internet Protection Act of 2000. Mr. Ogden filed an *amicus* brief arguing against Congress requiring public libraries that accept tax funding to install Internet filters, even on computers in the children's areas.
- Challenged the Child Protection and Obscenity Enforcement Act of 1988. Specifically, Mr. Ogden's brief on behalf of porn producers argued that requiring them to verify that performers were at least 18 years of age would "burden too heavily and infringe too deeply" on their First Amendment rights.
- Represented Playboy Enterprises in a 1986 suit that forced the Library of Congress to print *Playboy* magazine's articles in Braille, an outcome Mr. Ogden said was a key victory in "turning the tide in the censorship battle." He also sought an injunction against including *Playboy* in a list of porn magazines in the Meese Commission report (1990).
- Filed numerous briefs in other pornography and obscenity cases before the Supreme Court.
- Opposed parental notification for minors undergoing abortions (1987).

- Opposed virtually all restrictions on abortions, from spousal notification to mandatory 24-hour delays, in a brief for Planned Parenthood filed in the landmark U.S. Supreme Court case, *Casey v. Planned Parenthood* (1992).

- Characterized peaceful pro-life abortion protesters as the moral equivalent of mobsters by arguing they come under the RICO organized crime statute (*Scheidler v. National Organization for Women*, 2003).

- Declared that "homosexuality is a normal form of human sexuality" as counsel for the American Psychological Association in *Lawrence v. Texas* (2003), in which the Supreme Court struck down the Texas sodomy law. That profoundly bold judicial power grab has been the linchpin for further homosexual rights advances, including state court rulings striking down marriage laws in Massachusetts, California, and Connecticut.

- Sought to overturn the military's policy on service by open homosexuals (*Watkins v. United States Army*, 1989), arguing that sexual preference (sexual orientation) is the equivalent of race.

There's more. Mr. Ogden has backed the intrusion of international law into American courts (as occurred in the *Lawrence* case when majority opinion writer Justice Anthony Kennedy cited European opinions and reports as part of the ruling to overturn the Texas sodomy laws), the "right" of protesters to trespass on private property; the use of "compassion" to override "precedent and logic," and he has filed several briefs seeking to limit enforcement of the death penalty. His briefs are littered with junk science that was specifically designed to undermine cultural norms.

As deputy attorney general, the now-departed Mr. Ogden was sworn to defend the Constitution and the laws of the United States. That would have been a tall order for someone who has spent years inventing novel legal arguments in pursuit of a far-left social agenda.

CHAPTER 15

CHAI FELDBLUM
EQUAL EMPLOYMENT OPPORTUNITY COMMISSION

miss Feldblum is one of Obama's more dangerous appointees. She is smart, strategic and by being named as a commissioner at the Equal Employment Opportunity Commission (EEOC), which enforces federal civil rights laws, she is poised to impose on the American people the radical sexual agenda that she has advocated for years.

Feldblum, 50, is a Harvard Law grad and law professor at Georgetown University Law Center, where she has taught since 1991. An out lesbian, she has worked as an ACLU attorney on AIDS issues and clerked for Supreme Court Justice Harry Blackmun (author of the 1973 *Roe v. Wade* decision legalizing abortion).[241] She has been a leading force in redefining civil rights to go beyond traditional categories to include volitional sexual behavior via the recent psychological constructs known as "sexual orientation" and "gender identity." In essence, she believes that performing sodomy or engaging in cross-dressing entitles the practitioner to identical constitutional protective status under the law as religious belief, or being black, Hispanic,

Asian or white.

Her preferred vehicle is HR 3017, the Employment Non-Discrimination Act (ENDA),[242] a sweeping addition to civil rights law that would impose homosexuality and gender identity as new categories in workplace non-discrimination law. As of this writing, ENDA, whose primary sponsor in the House is Rep. Barney Frank (D-Mass.), was awaiting action in both houses of Congress. Earlier versions had passed each house in previous years but were removed in conference.

MAKING BIBLICAL NORMS BIGOTRY

This radical ENDA bill, for which Feldblum has been credited as an author, turns biblical sexuality into a form of bigotry punishable by law, and pastors into the equivalent of Bull Connor or the Ku Klux Klan, if they preach the full Word of God concerning sexuality. But it goes far beyond the clergy. ENDA affects all employers with 15 or more employees. The practical effect would be to kick religious liberties and conscience protection to the back of the bus and elevate homosexuality as a preferred category. This is already occurring in California, where state law forces employers to subsidize same-sex relationships or be barred from competing for state contracts. In effect, California's Christian businesspeople are being told to choose between God and Caesar if they want to stay in business.

Unlike many homosexual activists, Feldblum is quite blunt about the aim of the gay rights movement and its radical goals. She says civil rights are a "zero-sum" game, which will eventually yield this result: "Gays win, Christians lose."[243]

Observant Jews, Christians, and others who disapprove of homosexuality cannot say they haven't been warned. In an essay entitled "Moral Conflict and Liberty: Gay Rights and Religion,"[244] she poses this scenario:

> Now imagine that you and your opposite-sex wife have decided to open a Christian bed & breakfast. You view your guesthouse as a haven for God-fearing, evangelical Christians. You do not advertise generally on the Web, only on Christian sites. You make it very clear in all

Chai Feldblum
Newscom

your advertisements that you run a Christian business and that you will not rent rooms to cohabiting, homosexual couples (married or not) or to cohabiting, heterosexual couples who are not married. One day you are sued because your state has a law prohibiting discrimination based on marital status and sexual orientation. The court rules that the law places no burden on your religious beliefs because your religion does not require you to operate a guesthouse. You are ordered to change your guesthouse's rules.

No one can claim that the court order has prohibited you from "being religious." As the court has explained, you may continue to hold whatever beliefs you want about sexual practices. You simply may not impose those beliefs on others. But you feel that your beliefs and identity as a religious person simply cannot be disaggregated from your conduct. Your religious belief — your "belief liberty" interest, as I term it below — is necessarily curtailed by the *existence* of a law that prohibits you from discriminating on the basis of sexual orientation or marital status.

Although Feldblum, who was raised in an Orthodox Jewish household, voices some sympathy for the coming pain that conservative religious people will experience in the New Age of gay rights, she makes it clear that it's a necessary price.

She has not exactly been shy about her ambitions. At a seminar in 2004, she announced a "strategic plan" to bring about the gay agenda in the workplace this way:

> It requires the statement that "gay sex is morally good."...
> The idea is we want to change the American workplace

and we want to revolutionize social norms. This is a project that the Alfred P. Sloan Foundation is funding me to do — Workplace Flexibility 2010 ... we need legislative lawyering; policy research, and political and social engagement. And you need someone to fund and demand a three-year plan on each of those components. So here's my bottom line:

There is a war that needs to be fought. And it's not a war overseas, where we're killing people in the name of liberating them. It is a war right here at home, where we need to convince people that morality demands full equality for gay people.[245]

Feldblum has testified before Congress on behalf of the federal hate crimes bill and the Employment Non-Discrimination Act, which would elevate "sexual orientation" and "gender identity" to specially protected class status in the workplace. Since employers will try to avoid possible federal prosecution by hiring and promoting based on homosexual identity, some critics call ENDA the "gay quota" law.

The federal hate crimes bill was signed on October 28, 2009, by President Obama, and enforcement will fall largely to the Justice Department and to the EEOC, where Feldblum can use the power of her office to expand the reach of the homosexual agenda. The Matthew Shepard/James Byrd, Jr. Hate Crimes Prevention Act[246] greatly expands the power of the federal government to intervene in criminal cases, provides a $5 million annual slush fund of $100,000 grants for law enforcement and other organizations that promote the hate crimes concept, and introduces the un-American notions of unequal justice and "thought crimes" into the law. The law provides a foundation for legal assaults on the First Amendment freedoms of speech, religion, and assembly, despite some language that seemingly prohibits its misuse in these areas. This new law is a profoundly dangerous tool in the hands of social revolutionaries such as Miss Feldblum.

How revolutionary is her agenda? How about deconstructing marriage completely?

DISMANTLING MARRIAGE

Feldblum is a signer of the 2006 BeyondMarriage.org statement, "Beyond Same-Sex Marriage," which endorses all sexual relationships, from "gay" unions to polygamy. The document states:

LGBT communities have ample reason to recognize that families and relationships know no borders and will never slot narrowly into a single existing template.[247]

The document lists demands for recognition of relationships, including: "Committed, loving households in which there is more than one conjugal partner."

A letter sent to the U.S. Senate on Dec. 8, 2009, and signed by numerous pro-family groups opposing her nomination said this:

During her confirmation hearing, Feldblum attempted to distance herself from the radical statement, BeyondMarriage. She claimed it was a "mistake" to have signed this petition in 2006. Yet, she went on to say that she "agreed with the general thrust of the statement." While Feldblum denied supporting polygamy, she did not deny supporting polyamory, (multiple sex partners — both male and female).

The only mistake Feldblum made was getting caught. It was only the night before her confirmation hearing that she asked to have her name removed from the statement.

Here are just three of the bizarre positions in the BeyondMarriage statement:

- Committed, loving households in which there is more than one conjugal partner
- Queer couples who decide to jointly create and raise a child with another queer person or couple, in two households

- Marriage is not the only worthy form of family or relationship, and it should not be legally and economically privileged above all others.

Based on Feldblum's extensive writings and speeches, we know that she is a long-time supporter of government recognition of same-sex marriage and polyamorous relationships. She has stated:

- We want to change the American workforce and revolutionize social norms.... Our current public policies undermine the moral and political unit of same sex couples and families and that's a moral wrong that needs to be rectified.[248]
- I, for one, am not sure whether marriage is a normatively good institution. I have moved away from the belief that marriage is clearly the best normative way to structure intimate relationships, such that government should be actively supporting this social arrangement above all others.[249]

On March 27, 2010, President Obama named Feldblum as one of 15 "recess" appointees, skipping any Senate confirmation vote. The Obama Administration's willingness to put forth yet another fiercely radical advocate of the entire homosexual agenda is a promise kept to gay activists, who played a key role in building support for Mr. Obama and are an increasingly powerful force in his administration.

CHAPTER 16

ELENA KAGAN
U.S. SOLICITOR GENERAL AND
SUPREME COURT NOMINEE

O n May 10, 2010, President Obama nominated Elena Kagan to replace the retiring John Paul Stevens as an Associate Justice on the U.S. Supreme Court.

Kagan has been U.S. Solicitor General since March 2009. As the second most powerful legal authority, Kagan, 50, essentially guides federal legal initiatives. She has never been a judge, and has a thin paper trail. But her public record reveals a left-liberal outlook and a devotion to the idea of a "living Constitution" that allows infinite government expansion.

Legal expert Ken Klukowski, co-author of *The Blueprint: Obama's Plan to Subvert the Constitution and Build an Imperial Presidency*,[250] explains why Obama nominated Kagan:

> President Obama needs a Supreme Court that will rule that the Constitution allows the federal government to impose Obamacare's individual mandate, ordering

Americans how they must spend their own money. He needs a Supreme Court that will allow him to impose job-killing cap-and-trade and card-check through regulations, because he can't get them through Congress. He needs a Supreme Court that says you have a right to same-sex marriage and taxpayer-funded abortions—which the Constitution nowhere says—but that you have no right to own a gun—which the Constitution explicitly says in the Second Amendment.[251]

Kagan fills the bill. *Patriot Post* publisher Mark Alexander summarizes Kagan's appeal to Obama's talent scouts:

> While media profiles of Kagan paint her, predictably, as a moderate "consensus-builder," Kagan is, in fact, a genuine, hardcore Leftist, a former legal counsel to the Clintonista regime who began her political career in earnest as a staffer for liberal Massachusetts Governor Michael Dukakis's presidential run back in 1988.[252]

As Harvard Law School dean, she booted military recruiters off campus – during a time of war – because the armed forces do not allow open homosexuality. This stunning exhibition of skewed priorities alone should disqualify her for the Court.

She spoke to homosexual activist groups on campus that were pressing to overturn the military's homosexuality ban, and she filed a brief with the U.S. Supreme Court seeking to overturn the Solomon Amendment, which requires colleges accepting federal funds to allow military recruiters.

Nonetheless, even with this radical track record, she was affirmed by the U.S. Senate, 61 to 31, as Solicitor General with "yes" votes from seven Republicans, on March 19, 2009.

Responsible for all litigation on behalf of the United States in the Supreme Court and federal appellate courts, Kagan has enormous potential to help unravel the moral order. She could do infinitely more damage as a lifelong

Supreme Court justice. Even Arlen Specter (R-Pa. at the time, then D), who voted for porn attorney David Ogden as deputy attorney general, opposed her as Solicitor General. Given her relatively young age, she could project the left-liberalism represented by John Paul Stevens 30 to 40 years into the future.

A Harvard law school graduate, Kagan clerked for Judge Abner Mikva of the U.S. Court of Appeals for the District of Columbia after graduation and later for liberal Supreme Court Justice Thurgood Marshall.

Elena Kagan
Doc Searls

Ken Klukowski notes their pedigrees:

> Judge Abner Mikva was openly a far-left judge. And Justice Thurgood Marshall was the most liberal Supreme Court justice in American history, with ultra-left views on every single constitutional issue.[253]

Kagan practiced as a private attorney before becoming an assistant professor at the University of Chicago Law School. She worked in the White House for part of President's Clinton's term as Associate White House Counsel. She was also the deputy director of the Domestic Policy Council and Deputy Assistant to the President for Domestic Policy. She was on the Research Advisory Council of the Goldman Sachs Global Markets Institute from 2005 through 2008, *USA Today* reported.[254]

KAGAN VS. FREE SPEECH

In a 1996 paper, Kagan argued that the government may suppress speech if it is offensive to society or to the government.[255] Her approach basically turns the First Amendment on its head.

Legal analyst Horace Cooper explains:

> Kagan theorizes that the Courts – instead of focusing on the First Amendment's goal of ensuring that individual expression and the marketplace of ideas is encouraged – should focus on the government's motives in adopting regulations that impact speech. If their goals were neutral, then the impact on speech wouldn't necessarily be protected. Thus it would seem that as long as the government doesn't favor any given position on a topic, logically it could ban talk radio completely on public airwaves or ban all political campaigning using the Internet.[256]

As Solicitor General, Kagan argued in the U.S. government's brief[257] in *United States v. Stevens* that speech has no First Amendment protection, if harm outweighs benefits: "Whether a given category of speech enjoys First Amendment protection depends upon a categorical balancing of the value of the speech against its societal costs." The Court disagreed, and ruled on April 20 that the law, which outlawed depictions of animal cruelty, was unconstitutionally overbroad.

On the surface, this was a "hard case" involving a law barring the sale of videos depicting fatal dog fights and other depictions of animal cruelty. But the defendant was a 69-year-old animal lover who made videos of pit bulls fighting, in order to persuade people to stop the practice. In what was a clear government overreach, he had been sentenced to three years in prison, which is more than NFL star Michael Vick got for actually staging dog fights.[258]

Kagan's brief covers the allowable limitations of free speech, such as "fighting words," incitement to violence, obscenity, and others. The problem is that she opened a wider door to government determining the value of content. This could be applied down the road to "hate speech," which is becoming more broadly defined as more groups (such as homosexual activists and radical Muslims) take offense at negative portrayals.

The *Stevens* case is a part of a disturbing pattern, Cooper notes: "An examination of several of the law review articles she has written and the First Amendment cases in which she has involved herself as solicitor general reveals a consistent and inexplicable hostility toward free speech."[259]

In *Citizens United v. Federal Election Commission*,[260] the Supreme Court overturned the McCain-Feingold campaign financing restrictions that prohibited group-funded political ads within 30 days of a primary election. It was a huge victory for freedom of speech. The Federal Election Commission had barred the distribution and exhibition of a documentary film about Hillary Clinton during the presidential primary season. As Solicitor General, Kagan defended the Bipartisan Campaign Reform Act of 2002 (McCain-Feingold) statute (as she was required to do) but took it a step further, arguing that the law could ban books and even pamphlets during election season. Thomas Paine, call your office!

DEFENDING PARTIAL-BIRTH ABORTION

While serving in the White House, Kagan co-authored two memos to President Clinton in 1997 that offered a political strategy to defend his veto of the Senate ban on partial-birth abortion. Kagan's May 13, 1997, memo to Clinton, co-authored with her boss Bruce Reed, urged the President to support amendments to the ban offered by Sen. Tom Daschle and Sen. Dianne Feinstein as a means to "sustain your credibility on HR 1122 [Partial Birth Abortion Act] and prevent Congress from overriding your veto."[261]

Both the Daschle and Feinstein amendments applied after the baby was already viable and permitted partial-birth abortion if the health of the mother was at risk. Supporters of the ban derided both amendments as loopholes that would allow any and all partial-birth abortions because the U.S. Supreme Court defined the term "health" broadly in 1973 to include "all factors – physical, emotional, psychological, familial, and the woman's age – relevant to the well-being of the patient" (*Doe v. Bolton*[262]). In other words, a "health" exception under the Court's definition allows abortion at any time through all nine months of pregnancy for any reason.

Kagan's counsel was intended not to support a ban with exceptions, but to help insure that the Senate would not override the President's veto. National

Right to Life Committee legislative director Douglas Johnson told Lifenews. com, "The Daschle phony ban, which the Reed-Kagan memo endorses, had only one purpose, which was to provide political cover for pro-abortion senators who might otherwise feel compelled to vote to override President Clinton's veto of the Partial-Birth Abortion Ban Act. It was not a real ban, but a completely hollow political construct – all exception, no ban."[263]

The strategy, Johnson said, was "enough of a smokescreen to prevent the Senate from overriding Clinton's veto." A ban on the grisly procedure did not come until 2003 under President George W. Bush, a six-year delay for which, Johnson said, Kagan can claim some credit.

PRO-HOMOSEXUAL RECORD

After Clinton's presidency, Kagan became a professor at Harvard Law School and eventually the school's first woman dean. It was in that position that, in defiance of the Solomon Act, she supported not allowing military recruiters on campus because of her opposition to the military's "Don't Ask, Don't Tell" policy on homosexuality.

But she did more than that, observes Accuracy in Academia's Bethany Stotts, who writes that:

> Between 2003 and 2007, Dean Kagan not only used her position as Dean to encourage the academic community to protest military recruitment efforts, but was at rallies herself and appears to have coordinated her policy announcements with HLS Lambda, according to student news accounts at that time.
>
> HLS Lambda describes itself as "a social and political student organization dedicated to serving the lesbian, gay, bisexual, and transgender (LGBT) community at Harvard Law School," according to its website.[264]

In *F.A.I.R. v. Rumsfeld, et al*,[265] Kagan joined a legal brief with 52 other Harvard Law faculty in 2004 arguing against the Solomon Amendment, although she did not commit Harvard to be a plaintiff in the case. After that court ruled against the military, she immediately took action the next day against the recruiters, even though Harvard is not in the Third Circuit's jurisdiction. On March 6, 2006, the U.S. Supreme Court ruled unanimously (8-0) that military recruitment on college campuses did not violate the campus's free speech rights.

But Kagan continued her campaign against the military through her support of the campus homosexual activist group Harvard Law School Lambda, as Stott reports:

> Kagan continued to demonstrate her affinity with Lambda in 2007, and in 2008 reiterated her opposition to Don't Ask, Don't Tell.
>
> According to this transcript of the HLS Lambda's "Second Annual Gay and Lesbian Legal Advocacy Conference [on] 'Don't Ask, Don't Tell,'" held in March of 2007, Kagan was the moderator for the third panel, "The Contours of Judicial Deference to Military Personnel Policies."
>
> She says little, but the introductory remarks made by Alexis Caloza, "one of the political co-chairs" for the student group, are telling:
>
> "On a more personal note, I would like to thank Dean Kagan for her continuing support for the lesbian, gay, bisexual, and transgendered community here at Harvard. She has been a staunch critic of the Solomon Amendment, and in the months leading up to and following the Supreme Court's decision in *FAIR v. Rumsfeld*, she met regularly with students to discuss ways in which the Law School could help to ameliorate the harmful discriminatory effects of the Solomon Amendment and "Don't Ask, Don't Tell" generally.
>
> This conference would not have been possible without the tremendous support HLS Lambda received from Dean Kagan and her office...."[266]

JUDICIAL ACTIVIST

The people cited as heroes and role models tell a lot about a person's philosophy. A revealing moment occurred at Harvard Law School in 2006, in which Elena Kagan gave a brief speech before the presentation of the Peter Gruber Foundation Justice Prize.

Kagan praised Harvard Law grad and newly-retired President of the Supreme Court of Israel, Aharon Barak, as her "hero."[267]

Barak is a leftwing judicial activist whose legal philosophy goes beyond the limitations placed on the judiciary by the U.S. Constitution.

Barak said:

> According to my outlook, law fills the whole world. There is no sphere containing no law and no legal criteria. Every human act is encompassed in the world of law. Every act can be "imprisoned" within the framework of the law. Even actions of a clearly political nature, such as waging war, can be examined with legal criteria.[268]

This is an extension of the Left's propensity to see everything, even the personal, in a political context. Nothing, therefore, is truly private. Barak also advocates doing away with the need to show an "injury" in order to have standing in a case.

Barak wrote:

> I also favor expanding the rules of standing and releasing them from the requirement of an injury in fact. The Supreme Court of Israel has adopted this approach.[269]

The requirement to show an injury is an important aspect of U.S. jurisprudence. Otherwise, anyone could file nuisance lawsuits for whatever reason. Think for a moment about what a group like the ACLU could do, freed from having to find a plaintiff in order to attack a public expression of faith, such as a Ten Commandments obelisk. Can you say "harassment on steroids?"

SOFT SPOT FOR SOCIALISM

When she was a student at Princeton, Kagan wrote a 130-page thesis, "To the Final Conflict: Socialism in New York City, 1900-1933,"[270] which laments America's rejection of socialism and offers reasons. Here's a snippet:

> In our own times, a coherent socialist movement is nowhere to be found in the United States. Americans are more likely to speak of a golden past than of a golden future, of capitalism's glories than of socialism's greatness. (p. 127)

She went on to describe the demise of socialism in New York City as emblematic of the demise elsewhere:

> Granted that one city is not a nation, the experience of New York may yet suggest a new solution to this critical problem (p. 128).

"If Chief Justice John Roberts had written a thesis on fascism and opined that fascism had 'greatness' and described the Third Reich's 'demise' as a 'critical problem,' who would have said that it was irrelevant?" asks legal analyst Michael Gaynor, commenting on the media's kid-glove treatment of Kagan's thesis as a youthful indiscretion.[271]

And if there was any doubt as to her feelings about socialism's failure, she removed it with this:

> The story is a sad but also chastening one for those who, more than half a century after socialism's decline, still want to change America ... in unity lies their only hope (p. 130).

People can hope and change and grow, but Kagan's youthful, scholarly attempt to figure out what went wrong and how Americans might be attracted to piecemeal socialism in other guises is reminiscent of the view of socialist author and politician Upton Sinclair, who ran twice on the Socialist Party ticket for Congress and lost badly both times. He did better (although he still lost) when running as a Democrat for California governor in 1934 under the slogan: "End Poverty in California." In a letter to Socialist Party leader Norman Thomas, Sinclair wrote:

> The American People will take Socialism, but they won't take the label.[272]

Whether Elena Kagan would still be comfortable sporting that label, her writings and record would seem to fit comfortably into a socialist worldview — one advancing under the banner of "hope and change."

CHAPTER 17

ERIC H. HOLDER, JR.
U.S. ATTORNEY GENERAL

Eric Holder, 59, took office as Attorney General on Feb. 3, 2009, making him the first African-American to hold that post. His duties include giving legal advice to the President and the heads of the executive agencies, representing the United States in court, and overseeing the nation's 93 U.S. Attorneys.

A graduate of Columbia University (1973) and Columbia University Law School (1976), Holder clerked for the NAACP Legal Defense Fund and the Department of Justice's Criminal Division.[273] He went to work for the Public Integrity Section of the U.S. Justice Department from 1976 to 1988 before being named a D.C. Superior Court judge by President Ronald Reagan.[274] In 1993, Bill Clinton named him a U.S. Attorney for D.C., where he served until Clinton tapped him as deputy attorney general in 1997.[275] He also briefly served as Acting Attorney General under President George W. Bush, pending confirmation of John Ashcroft, whereupon Holder left for a job with a D.C. law firm. In 2007, he joined Barack Obama's campaign team as senior legal adviser. He was nominated in November 2008 as Attorney General and was confirmed by a vote of 75-21 by the U.S. Senate on February 2, 2009.[276]

From the start, Holder has generated controversy. Two weeks after being sworn in, he criticized his countrymen for not discussing racial matters more, calling America "a nation of cowards."[277] He also brought some baggage with him from his previous post as deputy attorney general under Bill Clinton. At the very end of his administration, in January 2001, Clinton signed a controversial pardon for Marc Rich, a major Clinton donor and commodities trader who had been indicted in 1983 on 65 counts, mostly on tax evasion. Rich had fled to Switzerland. As *Washington Post* columnist Richard Cohen relates,

> With the stroke of a pen, justice was not done. Holder was not just an integral part of the pardon process, he provided the White House with cover by offering his go-ahead recommendation.[278]

IGNORING A GROSS VIOLATION OF VOTING RIGHTS

Fast forward to May 2009. Holder's Justice Department inexplicably dropped charges against three New Black Panther Party members who had allegedly (and visibly – some of it was caught on videotape) harassed voters and a reporter in Philadelphia on Nov. 4, 2008[279] during the presidential election. One of the Panthers was wielding a billy club and yelling racial epithets. Despite a report from the U.S. Civil Rights Commission criticizing the inaction, Holder's Justice Department continued to ignore the case.

On May 14, 2010, J. Christian Adams, a Justice Department attorney, resigned, citing the handling of the Black Panther case. He and other attorneys had been subpoenaed by the Civil Rights Commission and were told to ignore them by Justice Department superiors, his letter of resignation states.[280]

On May 25, Judicial Watch, a public interest group that investigates and prosecutes government corruption, announced that it had filed a Freedom of Information Act (FOIA) lawsuit against the Justice Department to obtain documents related to the agency's decision to dismiss the claims against the New Black Panther Party for Self-Defense. Judicial Watch had originally filed a FOIA on June 18, 2009, but was met with bureaucratic stonewalling.[281]

In an editorial entitled "Special Protection for Black Panthers," *The Washington Times* noted that Holder, in scolding the nation upon taking office, vowed to "have frank conversations about the racial matters that continue to divide us." But the conversation appears to be one-sided. As the *Times* notes:

Eric Holder

The Holder Justice Department likewise argued mostly in favor of the town of New Haven, Conn., when it denied promotions to white firefighters who had earned them. Its new Civil Rights Division chief, Thomas Perez, made a point in his inaugural remarks of saying that the department's focus would be on protecting traditional minorities along with Muslim- and Arab-Americans, abortion doctors and "lesbian, gay, bisexual and transgendered individuals." The rights of others, though, got short shrift.[282]

KEY BACKER OF HOMOSEXUAL HATE CRIMES LAW

For years, Holder has supported the passage of the federal hate crimes legislation that includes "sexual orientation" and "gender identity," and which vastly expands the federal presence in criminal law enforcement. The law builds the foundation for similar measures that in Europe and Canada have resulted in suppressing the freedoms of religion, speech, and assembly.

As deputy attorney general, Holder first testified on behalf of a federal hate crimes law on July 8, 1998, before the Senate Judiciary Committee. A year later, on May 11, 1999, he did so again.[283] I was there as well, testifying on behalf of Family Research Council, opposing the law. Sen. Orrin Hatch (R-UT) asked Holder for evidence that law enforcement personnel were not routinely pursuing criminal charges against perpetrators of alleged hate crimes. Holder admitted that he had no hard evidence of this but promised to look some up.

By the way, the National Organization for (some) Women ripped my testimony, and said that my very *presence* as a witness was "an insult to the bill's sponsors and to the hundreds of religious, civil rights, law enforcement and other groups who support the legislation."[284] Hmm. Perhaps I was the victim of a hate crime.

Ten years later, on June 25, 2009, Holder again testified[285] before the Senate Judiciary Committee in support of the federal hate crimes bill, "The Matthew Shepard Hate Crimes Prevention Act of 2009," which Congress passed as a rider to a defense authorization bill, and which was signed into law by Obama on Oct. 28, 2009.[286] As *The Washington Times* reported, "President Obama delivered a major victory to the gay rights movement."[287]

SOFT SPOT FOR TERRORISTS?

In 1999, as deputy attorney general under Bill Clinton, Holder pushed his staff to drop their opposition to clemency for 16 members of Puerto Rican terror groups linked to bombings in New York, Chicago, and other locales during the 1970s and 1980s. According to a *Los Angeles Times* article about documents released in 2009:

> President Clinton's decision to commute prison terms caused an uproar at the time. Holder was called before Congress to explain his role but declined to answer numerous questions from angry lawmakers demanding to know why the Justice Department had not sided with the FBI, federal prosecutors, and other law enforcement officials, who were vehemently opposed to the grants....

Holder instructed his staff at Justice's Office of the Pardon Attorney to effectively replace the department's original report recommending against any commutations, which had been sent to the White House in 1996, with one that favored clemency for at least half the prisoners, according to these interviews and documents.[288]

CONFUSING TERRORISTS WITH CRIMINAL DEFENDANTS

In November 2009, Holder announced plans to bring from Guantanamo Bay confessed 9/11 mastermind Khalid Sheikh Mohammed, and Al-Qaeda terrorist suspects Ramzi Bin al-Shibh, Walid bin Attash, Mustafa Ahmed al-Hawsawi and Ali Abdul Aziz and put them on trial in U.S. criminal courts in New York City. Until then, terrorists were tried in military tribunals. American Civil Rights Union legal fellows Ken Blackwell and Ken Klukowski describe Holder's plan as legally incomprehensible, politically naïve, and:

> ... perhaps liberals' worst idea in years. KSM and his cohorts had agreed to plead guilty before a military tribunal, accept a sentence of death, and speedily rendezvous with their 72 ladies-in-waiting.
>
> This offer of an efficient way out for the administration was not good enough for Attorney General Eric Holder. He insists on trying the terrorists before a civilian jury in federal court, just a few hundred yards from Ground Zero. Next to martyrdom and a free trip to paradise, this has to be the terrorists' wildest dream.[289]

The major flaw here is treating these cases as if they are run-of-the-mill criminal offenses instead of terrorism. With criminal cases, prosecutors and police try to collect evidence to secure a conviction. In a terror case, prosecution is an afterthought; the main objective is to get information to prevent a terrorist attack. As such, invoking the rules of evidence for a criminal case is absurd when investigators are working feverishly to prevent a tragedy, not thinking about how a jury might view the evidence. Also, many terrorists, who are regarded as "enemy combatants," are captured in combat conditions. Treating them like burglars or car jackers makes no sense. That's why military tribunals have a less stringent standard for admitting evidence.

Many of these errors in judgment might be driven by officials' attempts to appease radical Muslims and to align themselves with President Obama's Muslim sympathies.

At a November 18, 2009, Senate Judiciary Committee hearing, when pressed by Sen. Lindsey Graham (R-SC) to say whether he would rule out Osama bin Laden being tried in a civilian court and given Miranda warnings, Holder repeatedly refused to do so.[290]

On May 13, 2010, during a House Judiciary Committee hearing, Rep. Lamar Smith (R-TX) asked Holder several times if "radical Islam" was at least one factor in terrorist incidents such as the Fort Hood massacre, the Detroit airline "underwear" bomber, and the Times Square near-bombing by Faisal Shahzad. Here's a summary from Fox News:

> "There are a variety of reasons why I think people have taken these actions," Holder told the House Judiciary Committee. "One, I think, just look at each individual case. We are in the process now of talking to Mr. (Faisal) Shahzad to try to understand what it is that drove him to take the action."
>
> The question as to whether the individuals were incited by radical Islam came from the committee's ranking member Rep. Lamar Smith (R-Texas).
>
> Smith followed, "But radical Islam could have been one of the reasons?"
>
> Holder again said, "There are a variety of reasons."
>
> Smith later asked, "But all I'm asking is do you think among those variety of reasons, radical Islam might have been one of the reasons that the individuals took the steps that they did?" After a two-minute back and forth, Holder eventually said, "I certainly think that it's possible that people who espouse a radical version of Islam have had an ability to have an impact on people like Mr. Shahzad."[291]

Ken Blackwell, author and former Secretary of State of Ohio, says some government officials – like Holder – are becoming de facto "dhimmicrats." Dhimmitude is the second-class status accorded to non-Muslims in Muslim majority nations. Blackwell writes:

> It's not the same thing as a Democrat. A dhimmicrat is a person who, while not Muslim himself, nonetheless clears the path for shariah law to be adopted and incorporated into otherwise free nations.... Eric Holder is a leading dhimmicrat in government today. Our Attorney General has yet to rule out a civilian trial in Manhattan for Khalid Sheikh Muhammad, the mastermind of the 9/11 attacks. Khalid Sheikh Muhammad boasted of how he beheaded *Wall Street Journal* reporter Danny Pearl. A more loathsome human being would be hard to imagine. But Eric Holder is giving Khalid Sheikh Muhammad all the rights accorded to American citizens accused of mass murder. Why? Why, too, should Farouk Abdul Mutallab, the Christmas Day underwear bomber, be given a Miranda warning and allowed to escape trial before a military tribunal? Our A.G. has no coherent answer to these questions.[292]

ASSAILING ARIZONA FOR ENFORCING FEDERAL IMMIGRATION LAW

In May 2010, Holder was one of several Obama Administration officials who sharply criticized the state of Arizona for passing a law to enforce federal immigration rules. Holder threatened to sue state officials, and told ABC News's *This Week* that "we could potentially get on a slippery slope where people will be picked on because of how they look as opposed to what they have done."[293] He was echoing the sentiments of his boss, Barack Obama, who warned on April 27, that "... suddenly if you don't have your papers and you took your kid out to get ice cream, you're going to be harassed, that's something that could potentially happen."[294]

Obama and Holder ignored portions of the law that bar racial profiling and that allow an immigration check only as part of "any lawful stop, detention or arrest."[295] In other words, someone cannot be stopped simply because they appear to be of Mexican heritage; officers must have a good reason.

At a May 14, 2010 House Judiciary Committee hearing, when Rep. Ted Poe (R-TX) asked him whether he had read the law, Holder replied, "I have not had a chance to – I've glanced at it." Poe helpfully said, "I'll give you my copy of it if you would like."[296] That would be easy. It's only 10 pages.

BLAME GAME IN THE GULF

On June 1, 2010, Holder made a well-publicized trip to the Gulf of Mexico, threatening criminal action against BP. Holder's photo-op came as the company struggled to contain the oil gushing from 5,000 feet below where an oil platform mysteriously blew up two days before Earth Day, on April 20, 2010, killing 11 and causing one of the worst environmental disasters in U.S. history.

In a way, Holder's visit strengthens the perception that the Obama Administration thinks that any problem can be handled through a consensus solution dreamed up by Ivy League faculty. Instead of sending tankers to sop up the oil or barges to build barrier islands, as Louisiana Gov. Bobby Jindal pleaded for them to do, they sent – lawyers.

CHAPTER 18

MORE APPOINTEES, MORE LEFTIST VIEWS

P resident Obama still has posts to fill as of this writing, but the people he has already chosen reflect a bias toward secular, leftist appointments.

Here are some brief sketches of more appointees.

SONIA SOTOMAYOR
ASSOCIATE JUSTICE, UNITED STATES SUPREME COURT

Sonia Sotomayor, 55, was appointed to the Supreme Court on May 26, 2009, and confirmed by the Senate on August 6, 2009, by a vote of 68 to 31.

Obama had said that he wanted to appoint judges that ruled not only with an understanding of the law but through "empathy" for disadvantaged people. In practice, this could mean ignoring the law and tipping the scale based on the whims of the judge. Based on her decisions, Sotomayor's appointment appears to meet Obama's requirement of law based on feelings and empowerment. But for the most powerless of all — unborn babies — Sotomayor does not have a strong track record.

From 1980 until 1992, Sotomayor served on the board – at times as vice president and chairman of the litigation committee – of the Puerto Rican Legal Defense and Education Fund. *The New York Times* in 1992 described her as "a top policy maker on the board" at a time when the fund filed briefs in six court cases on behalf of "abortion rights."[297]

In *Ohio v. Akron Center*, the fund wrote that it "opposes any efforts to overturn or in any way restrict the rights recognized in *Roe v. Wade*," which would mean opposing even widely supported laws such as bans on partial birth abortion and taking minors across state lines for abortions without parental knowledge.[298]

Sotomayor also has shown a willingness to support racial preferences. As part of a three-judge panel of the 2nd Circuit appeals court, Sotomayor upheld the city of New Haven's rejection of a discrimination lawsuit in *Ricci v. DeStefano* by white firefighters and one Hispanic who were denied promotions solely on the basis of race. The Supreme Court overruled that decision.

She also said, "I would hope that a wise Latina woman with the richness of her experiences would more often than not reach a better conclusion than a white male who hasn't lived that life."[299]

KATHLEEN SEBELIUS
SECRETARY OF HEALTH AND HUMAN SERVICES

Pro-family activists in Kansas, where Sebelius, 61, was governor, will tell you that she is one of the most wiley and tenacious supporters of abortion in the nation. Sebelius ran into some momentary problems with her nomination when it was revealed that she had understated donations to her campaign by the late George Tiller, once the nation's most notorious late-term abortionist. Sebelius, who supports late-term, or partial-birth abortion, vetoed several bills restricting abortion, including even two bills requiring abortion clinics to abide by typical medical clinic safety regulations.[300]

Sebelius also has spoken at Planned Parenthood functions and enthusiastically backs the sweeping government takeover of health care. As Secretary of Health and Human Services (HHS), Sebelius controls a $700 billion budget and stands to gain the most power from the proposed federal health care takeover.

In September 2009, HHS issued a naked threat against the insurance giant Humana for a letter that Humana sent its customers warning of complications posed by the health care bill.[301] The HHS letter indicated that Humana or any other insurance company that didn't play along would be dropped from the Medicare Advantage plans if it did not desist:

> We are instructing you to immediately discontinue all such mailings, and remove any related materials from your Web sites.[302]

DAVID HAMILTON
JUDGE, SEVENTH U.S. CIRCUIT COURT OF APPEALS

Known best as the U.S. District judge who enjoined the Indiana House in 2005 from allowing a pastor to mention the name of Jesus in an opening prayer at the Indiana legislature, Hamilton, on the other hand, approved the mention of Allah.

As *National Review*'s Ed Whelan comments:

> One peculiar aspect of Hamilton's ruling is how he drew the line between "sectarian" and "non-sectarian" prayers. On the one hand, Hamilton made clear that prayers that "use Christ's name or title" are sectarian. On the other hand, he ruled (on a post-judgment motion) that it is presumptively not sectarian for a Muslim imam to offer a prayer to "Allah"[303]

Hamilton, 52, also has a pro-abortion record. Marjorie Dannenfelser of the Susan B. Anthony List said,

> For seven years on the bench as a federal district judge, Hamilton prevented the implementation of Indiana's informed consent law, a measure enacted by the Indiana state legislature in line with precedent set by *Planned*

149

Parenthood v. Casey. The law established that at least 18 hours before an abortion, doctors must explain the risks and alternatives to abortion, as well as offer women the opportunity to see an ultrasound picture of their child and hear the infant's heartbeat.[304]

Sen. Jeff Sessions (R-Ala.), the ranking Judiciary Committee member, challenged the nomination, saying,

President Obama chose to set an aggressive tone by nominating Judge David Hamilton, a former board member and vice president for litigation of the Indiana chapter of the ACLU, as his first nominee.[305]

Sessions noted that Hamilton's "nomination is clearly controversial," and said that Hamilton has "drive[n] a political agenda," embracing the "empathy standard [and] the idea of a living Constitution."[306] Hamilton was confirmed by the Senate, 59-39, on November 19, 2009, with the sole Republican yes vote provided by Indiana's Richard Lugar.

NANCY SUTLEY
CHAIRMAN OF THE COUNCIL ON ENVIRONMENTAL QUALITY

Sutley, 47, who held a variety of environmental posts in Southern Caliornia, was a member of Hillary Clinton's California Lesbian, Gay, Bisexual and Transgender primary steering committee. She was confirmed on a unanimous Senate vote on January 22, 2009.[307]

Sutley, who was an official in the Environmental Protection Agency during the Clinton years, "is the first prominent gay person to earn a senior role in Obama's new administration," according to Wikipedia.[308]

Sutley accompanied the U.S. delegation to the Copenhagen Climate Change conference in early December 2009.

In July, England's left-leaning *Guardian* had interviewed her and wrote:

Nancy Sutley, who is pivotal in setting Obama's green

agenda as the chairwoman of the White House Council on Environmental Quality, told the *Guardian* that the president is ready to use his considerable personal popularity to rally Congress behind a sweeping climate change bill.

"When the bill is further along in the legislative process, there are some things where it may make a difference in expressing a strong view," Sutley said in an interview. "What [Obama] has been saying consistently is that he wants a bill and that this represents a very important step forward."[309]

M. JOHN BERRY
DIRECTOR, OFFICE OF PERSONNEL MANAGEMENT

The Office of Personnel Management (OPM) oversees human resources and benefits policies for 1.9 million federal employees and 2.5 million retirees and survivor annuitants. Prior to his OPM appointment, Berry, 50, was director of the National Zoo, where he supported various pro-homosexual policies. The openly gay Berry has moved quickly to bring that movement's agenda to bear on the federal workforce.

On November 18, 2009, Berry threw his support behind committee passage of a House bill sponsored by lesbian Rep. Tammy Baldwin (D-Wis.) that would extend marital-type domestic partner benefits to federal employees' same-sex partners. In an OPM press release, Berry said:

> President Obama has stated clearly that this is an issue of equality. But just as important, youth today, LGBT or not, see this benefit as a litmus test for determining high quality employers. The Administration looks forward to continuing its work with lawmakers as the House and the Senate move toward enactment of this bill.[310]

On June 1, 2010, Berry announced that same-sex partners would be eligible for long-term disability benefits. On June 2, 2010, Obama announced that a whole range of marital-type benefits, including adoption counseling, access to fitness facilities, medical treatment, credit unions, hardship transfer considerations, and several others would be extended to same-sex partners. In a June 2 memorandum, Berry ordered all executive agencies to implement the new policies.[311] The move is a blatant bypassing of the federal Defense of Marriage Act,[312] which defines marriage for all federal purposes as the union of one man and one woman.

In a press release, Berry hailed the moves: "This is another major step forward for gay and lesbian federal employees."[313]

DAWN JOHNSEN
NOMINEE, ASSISTANT ATTORNEY GENERAL

Johnsen, 48, was nominated in January 2009 to run the Office of Legal Counsel, but withdrew her nomination on April 9, 2010.[314] Johnsen was a staff counsel for the ACLU and legal director for the National Abortion and Reproductive Rights Action League (NARAL). In 1989, in a friend of the court brief in *Webster v. Reproductive Health Services*, Johnsen equated having a baby with slavery:

> Statutes that curtail [a woman's] abortion choice are disturbingly suggestive of involuntary servitude, prohibited by the Thirteenth Amendment in that forced pregnancy requires a woman to provide continuous physical service to the fetus in order to further the state's asserted interest.[315]

As *The Washington Times* observed in an editorial:

> The Thirteenth Amendment to the Constitution abolished slavery in 1865. The statute Ms. Johnsen opposed was written to limit public funding for abortions. It takes a questionable leap in logic to argue that involuntary servitude results from taxpayer funds not being used for abortion. Even if a woman cannot afford an abortion, the choice to have sex was her own, and that involved the

possibility of getting pregnant. Taxpayers had nothing to do with her sexual choices and are not enslaving her by preferring that their money not be used to end her baby's life.[316]

The Times also noted that during her hearing, Johnsen denied that she had ever made a Thirteenth Amendment argument, and had made other claims that lacked evidence. The Senate Judiciary Committee twice approved her nomination, but amid threats of a Republican filibuster, and several Democrats indicating they might join it, Johnsen finally withdrew her nomination.[317]

THOMAS PERRELLI
ASSOCIATE ATTORNEY GENERAL

Mr. Perrelli was the lawyer for Michael Schiavo, who had his brain-damaged wife Terri taken off life support against the wishes of her brother and parents. Perrelli, 43, who had been a deputy assistant attorney general during the Clinton Administration, was confirmed by the Senate in a 72-20 vote on March 12, 2009.

In March 2005, just weeks before Mrs. Schiavo died, Congress passed a bill, signed by President Bush, allowing her family to take its case from state courts to federal courts in an effort to stop the euthanasia. Perrelli was part of the team advising opponents during the proceedings.[318]

LifeNews' Steven Ertelt noted that Obama now regrets his role in the effort to give Mrs. Schiavo's family the federal court option:

> During his debate with Hillary Clinton in the Democratic presidential primary, Obama said his biggest mistake was voting with a unanimous Senate to help save Terri.[319]

As the No. 3 Justice Department official, Perrelli approved dropping charges in May 2009 against three New Black Panther Party members who had been videotaped allegedly harassing voters and a reporter outside a Philadelphia polling place on election day in November 2008.[320] The decision to drop the case caused outrage, especially since, as *The Washington*

Times explains:

> The department's career lawyers in the Voting Section
> of the Civil Rights Division, who pursued the complaint
> for five months, had recommended that Justice seek
> sanctions against the party and three of its members
> after the government had already won a default judgment
> in federal court against the men.[321]

EPILOGUE

TAKE HEART

n closing ... take heart. On May 27, 2009, President Obama spoke at major fundraisers on the West Coast. In the Hollywood event, he recited a litany of radical changes that his administration and Congress had already made in merely four months, from massive economic "stimulus" spending to expanding government health insurance for children to lifting the ban on embryonic stem cell research and nominating Sonia Sotomayor to the Supreme Court.

To thunderous applause, he punctuated it all by saying,

> Take heart in the change we've already brought. But I want you to know, Los Angeles, that you ain't seen nothing yet.[322]

Indeed. Virtually every day has brought new overtures of bigger and bigger government, takeovers of entire segments of the economy, direct attacks on the moral order of marriage and family, and evermore fawning media coverage.

But you can fool the people only so long. There is growing evidence that the Left has overreached and awakened a sleeping giant. Millions of Americans, including many independents, have come to realize that their nation has been seized by a radical elite backed by a "drive by" media, as Rush Limbaugh calls the press. Far from being discouraged, many have turned to alternative media and have begun organizing to take their country back.

The TEA Party movement, which began to gel on April 15, 2009, with rallies around the nation, surged into a massive rally on the Mall at the Capitol on Sept. 12, with crowd estimates ranging up to 1.5 million. One of the most encouraging of the thousands of signs was the one held by an older woman that read: "First Time Protester: I'm Off the Sidelines." Throughout the high-spirited crowd, the bright yellow Gadsden "Don't Tread on Me" flag could be seen waving in the breeze.

Later, on Nov. 5, a rally opposing the government takeover of health care attracted up to 20,000 people only a few days after Rep. Michele Bachman (R-Minn.) and some conservative talk show hosts gave a call to action. Bachman, who has become a favorite target of the liberal media, but a heroine to the growing Resistance, took to the floor of the House of Representatives on June 9, 2009. She declared boldly that the billions of dollars in the takeover of the auto industry and subsequent "favors" by powerful lawmakers to desperate car dealers amounted to "gangster government."[323]

Cracks are appearing in the Obama media-fed imperial presidency, and they are coming from unlikely chisels. In September 2009, two young conservatives, James O' Keefe and Hannah Giles, stunned the world by releasing videos of their posing as a pimp and prostitute at several ACORN offices on both coasts, where ACORN employees counseled them on how to break the law and even how to run a brothel with underage, trafficked girls. Although the media tried to ignore it for days, pressure built as the footage was gradually released by Breitbart.tv and Fox's *The Glenn Beck Show*. It caused such an uproar that both houses of Congress voted to halt funding to ACORN. But the biggest loser was the media, which had once again been exposed as so liberal that they would try to ignore a major and colorful scandal in order to shield a radical organization with close ties to the Obama Administration.

VOTERS SEND A MESSAGE

Off-year elections in 2009 gave further evidence that something is brewing. The gubernatorial victories of pro-life GOP candidates Chris Christie in New Jersey and Robert McDonnell in Virginia jolted the political establishment. New Jersey is a heavily unionized Democratic stronghold, and incumbent Jon Corzine spent millions of his own money. McDonnell's 17-point victory margin in Virginia over Creigh Deeds came despite a pre-election *Washington Post* series on a term paper McDonnell wrote on family values during his graduate school days. Virginians shrugged and sent the *Post* — and the country — a message. In New York's 23rd District, conservative candidate Doug Hoffman knocked out the liberal Republican Dede Scozzafava, allowing Democrat Bill Owens to take temporary ownership of the congressional seat, with another election coming in 2010. Both Hoffman and Owens oppose "gay marriage," unlike Scozzafava, who had embraced a liberal policy agenda.

In a December 2009 state Senate election in Kentucky, victorious GOP candidate Jimmy Higdon won by "nationalizing" the election and tying his opponent to Nancy Pelosi and the government health care takeover bill.[324]

The big hammer fell on January 19, 2010, however, when Republican upstart candidate Scott Brown won the Massachusetts Senate seat formerly held by Ted Kennedy for four decades. This addition of a 41st Republican Senate vote eliminated the Democrats' ability to end GOP filibusters. ObamaCare was the major issue.

And despite the closed-door (and possibly illegal) creation by Senate Majority Leader Harry Reid and House Speaker Nancy Pelosi of the massive, 2,733-plus page government health care takeover bill that Obama signed into law on March 23, 2010, support for ObamaCare continues to drop and Congress continues to get an earful from constituents.

As Americans learn more about what the Left has in mind for them and their children and grandchildren, the façade of a centrist "hope and change" agenda is collapsing. Polls are finicky things, so it's not good to get either too excited or too discouraged by surveys. However, the Obama team cannot be happy about his steadily falling approval ratings. On March 31, 2010, only

33 percent "strongly approved" of his leadership, with 41 percent "strongly disapproving." Among independents, only 19 percent "strongly approved" with 45 percent "strongly disapproving."[325]

STRUGGLE FOR NATION'S SOUL

In 1994, after Republicans stunned the nation by taking control of both houses of Congress after being in the minority for 40 years, ABC News anchor Peter Jennings expressed the disgust of many colleagues in the media by angrily accusing the electorate of being

> ... a nation full of uncontrolled two-year-old rage.... The voters had a temper tantrum last week.... Parenting and governing don't have to be dirty words.[326]

The '94 "tantrum" was a political revolt that did not last. The revolution that is brewing today against the Left's massive power grab may go much deeper, however, as Americans work to recommit our social and political institutions to the values of a free republic. This is about far more than two political parties battling it out. It's about a nation struggling to recover its animating principles — and its very soul.[327]

When you hear people who have been politically apathetic say things like, "We've got one more chance to save our country," and congressional leaders likening TEA Party protesters to Nazis, you know something more important than mere politics is at work.

America's founders, who created the Constitution as a way to keep government as our servant and not the other way around, would be appalled at a lot of things today. The sheer size of the federal government would astound Madison, Jefferson and Washington. So, too, would the sophistry and dishonesty of cultural elites, as they go about brazenly replacing a free republic with a confiscatory, centralized socialist system. But only a people schooled in truth, history, and logic can see through the seductive lies that socialists spin in the name of "fairness," "tolerance," and "equality."

Along with a rebirth of political activism toward limited government, Americans may well rediscover the source and inspiration for our nation's love of liberty.

In *The Book That Made America*," Dr. Jerry Newcombe makes a powerful case that without a common understanding of the Bible and God's providence, America could not have become the beacon of freedom to the world, and that it cannot long remain free without it. In fact, Dr. Newcombe contends that in the end, America is in the midst of a spiritual battle that might well result in a bright future.

"The late Dr. D. James Kennedy used to say that the only thing that can really change America for the better is true revival," Newcombe writes. "The first Great Awakening, of course, helped lead to the founding of America. The Second Great Awakening helped lead to the end of the evil of slavery. Now, we need a Third Great Awakening."[328]

America's chapters are not all written. The next few years could prove to be among the most exciting in our nation's history. There is little that is more exhilarating than recovering something that was lost.

With God's help and millions of people coming off the sidelines, we just might be able to leave our children and grandchildren feeling even more blessed than the generations that came before.

So, take heart. No more hand-wringing. Let's all get busy.

ENDNOTES

1   Can be viewed on YouTube at: http://www.youtube.com/watch?v=xvJJP9AYgqU.

2   Jake Tapper, "Spread the Wealth?" ABCNews.com, Oct. 14, 2008, at: http://blogs.abcnews.
com/politicalpunch/2008/10/spread-the-weal.html.

3   Julia Seymour, "NY Times 'Spotlights' Joe the Plumber with Left-Wing Attacks,"
Newsbusters.org, Media Research Center, Oct. 16, 2008, at: http://newsbusters.org/blogs/
julia-seymour/2008/10/16/ny-times-blog-spotlights-joe-plumber-left-wing-attacks.

4   Colleen Raezler and Brian Fitzpatrick, "How the TV Networks Have Portrayed Sarah Palin
as Dunce or Demon," Culture and Media Institute, Media Research Center, October 2008,
at: http://www.cultureandmediainstitute.org/specialreports/2008/SarahPalinChar/
SaraPalinExec_Sum.htm.

5   Rich Noyes, "Obama's Margin of Victory: The Media," Media Research Center, at: http://www.
mrc.org/SpecialReports/2008/obama/obama.asp.

6   Kyle Drennen, "Newsweek's Evan Thomas: Obama Is 'Sort of God,'" Newsbusters.org,
June 5, 2009 at: http://newsbusters.org/blogs/kyle-drennen/2009/06/05/newsweek-s-
evan-thomas-obama-sort-god.

7   Brad Wilmouth, "Matthews: Obama Speech Caused 'Thrill Going Up My Leg,'" Newsbusters.
org, at: http://newsbusters.org/blogs/brad-wilmouth/2008/02/13/matthews-obama-
speech-caused-thrill-going-my-leg.

8   "AFTAH: Folsom Street Fair in Speaker Nancy Pelosi's District with Its Public Nudity and
Street Orgies Represents America's Deepening Moral Crisis," Americans for Truth,
Sept. 26, 2008, at: http://americansfortruth.com/news/aftah-folsom-street-fair-in-
speaker-nancy-pelosi%e2%80%99s-district-with-its-public-nudity-and-street-orgies-
represents-america%e2%80%99s-deepening-%e2%80%98moral-crisis%e2%80%99.html.

9   "Fannie Mae's Patron Saint," editorial, The Wall Street Journal, Sept. 9, 2008, at: http://online.
wsj.com/article/SB122091796187012529.html.

10   C-Span2 clips can be viewed here: http://www.youtube.com/watch?v=_MGT_cSi7Rs. Barney Frank
is at 4:53 to 5:03 and again at 6:05 to 6:15.

11   Ibid., at 41 to 60 seconds into the video.

12   Melissa G. Pardue, "Waxman Report Is Riddled with Errors, Inaccuracies," The Heritage
Foundation, Memo #615, Dec. 2, 2004, at: http://www.heritage.org/Research/Abstinence/
wm615.cfm.

13   Sharon Kehnemui Liss, "Durbin Apologizes for Nazi, Gulag, Pol Pot Remarks," FoxNews.com, June
22, 2005, at: http://www.foxnews.com/story/0,2933,160275,00.html.

14   Victor Davis Hanson, "Where Did These Guys Come From?" Pajamasmedia, Dec. 23, 2009, at:
http://pajamasmedia.com/victordavishanson/where-did-these-guys-come-from/2/.

15   Cliff Kincaid, "The Blogger Who Nailed Van Jones," Accuracy in Media, Sept. 7, 2009, at: http://
www.aim.org/aim-column/the-blogger-who-nailed-van-jones.

16   Thomas Sowell, "The Dismantling of America, Piece by Piece," Investors.com, Oct. 27, 2009, at:
http://www.investors.com/NewsAndAnalysis/Article.aspx?id=510520.

17   Michael Scherer, "Calling 'Em Out: The White House Takes on the Press," *TIME* magazine, Oct. 8, 2009, at: http://www.time.com/time/politics/article/0,8599,1929058,00.html.

18   David Carr, "The Battle Between the White House and Fox News," *The New York Times*, Oct. 17, 2009, at: http://www.nytimes.com/2009/10/18/weekinreview/18davidcarr.html?_r=2.

19   Anita Dunn, in clip from Pajamasmedia.com and aired on Oct. 16, 2009, on *The Glenn Beck Show* on Fox News Channel: http://pajamasmedia.com/rogerkimball/2009/10/16/a-maoist-in-the-white-house/ at 35 to 47, then 1:16 to 1:46.

20   "Obama aide fires back at Beck over Mao remarks," CNN, Oct. 16, 2009, at: http://www.cnn.com/2009/POLITICS/10/16/beck.dunn/index.html#cnnSTCVideo.

21   Robert Knight, "Shielding Obama From the Power of Ridicule," Townhall.org, June 5, 2008, at: http://townhall.com/columnists/RobertKnight/2008/06/05/shielding_obama_from_the_power_of_ridicule.

22   Robert Knight and Colleen Raezler, *Character the Most Important Issue in the Presidential Primary Debates*, Special Report, Culture and Media Institute, Media Research Center, 2008, p. 15, at: http://www.cultureandmediainstitute.org/specialreports/2008/Character/CharacterFull_Report.htm.

23   Ibid., p. 22.

24   Viveca Novak and Brooks Jackson, "'He Lied' About Bill Ayers?," FactCheck.org, Annenberg Public Policy Center, Oct. 10, 2008, at: http://www.factcheck.org/elections-2008/he_lied_about_bill_ayers.html.

25   Richard Henry Lee, "Obama and the Woods Fund of Chicago," American Thinker, July 7, 2008, at: http://www.americanthinker.com/2008/07/obama_and_the_woods_fund_of_ch.html.

26   Linda Harvey, "Bill Ayers' 'gay' agenda for your kids," WorldNetDaily.com, Oct. 13, 2008, at: http://www.wnd.com/index.php?pageId=77640.

27   Bernardine Dohrn, Northwestern Law website at: http://www.law.northwestern.edu/faculty/profiles/BernardineDohrn/.

28   FactCheck.org, op. cit.

29   FactCheck.org, op. cit.

30   Stanley Kurtz, "Inside Obama's Acorn: By their fruits ye shall know them," *National Review Online*, May 29, 2008, at: http://article.nationalreview.com/print/?q=NDZiMjkwMDczZWI5ODdjOWYxZTIzZGIyNzEyMjE0ODDI=.

31   Barack Obama, The White House, at: http://www.whitehouse.gov/administration/president-obama/

32   A photocopy of the registration document is available by scrolling down at Occidental College, Snopes.com at: http://www.snopes.com/politics/obama/birthers/occidental.asp.

33   Ibid.

34   "Early life and career of Barack Obama," Wikipedia, at: http://en.wikipedia.org/wiki/Early_life_and_career_of_Barack_Obama.

35   Ibid.

36   Trevor Loudon, "Barack Obama's Marxist Mentor," NewZeal.blogspot.com, March 29, 2007, at: http://newzeal.blogspot.com/2007/03/barack-obamas-marxist-mentor.html.

37   Ibid.

38   Herb Romerstein, "Communism in Hawaii and the Obama Connection," USASurvival.org, at: http://74.125.93.132/search?q=cache:bs41XKPrneIJ:www.usasurvival.org/docs/hawaii-obama.pdf+herb+romerstein+hawaii&cd=3&hl=en&ct=clnk&gl=us.

39   Cliff Kincaid, "Obama's Communist Mentor," Accuracy in Media, Feb. 18, 2008, at: http://www.aim.org/aim-column/obamas-communist-mentor/.

40   Ibid.

41   Barack Obama, *Dreams from My Father (New York:* Three Rivers Press, 2004 revised edition), p. 98.

42   Ibid., p. 97.

43   Ibid., p. 100.

44   Cliff Kincaid, "Obama's Communist Mentor."

45   Cliff Kincaid, "Communism in Hawaii and the Obama Connection," USA Survival, Inc. at: http://74.125.93.132/search?q=cache:bs41XKPrneIl:www.usasurvival.org/docs/hawaii-obama.pdf+herb+romerstein+hawaii&cd=3&hl=en&ct=clnk&gl=us.

46   Ibid.

47   Cliff Kincaid, "Obama's Red Mentor Praised Red Army," Accuracy in Media, April 30, 2008, at: http://www.aim.org/aim-report/obamas-red-mentor-praised-red-army/.

48   Ibid.

49   Ben Smith and Jeffrey Ressner, "Exclusive: Obama's lost law review article," *Politico,* August 22, 2008, at: http://www.politico.com/news/stories/0808/12705.html.

50   Seth Stern, "A Commander in Chief," *Harvard Law Bulletin,* Fall 2008, at: http://www.law.harvard.edu/news/bulletin/2008/fall/feature_1.php.

51   Peter Slevin, "For Clinton and Obama, a Common Ideological Touchstone," *The Washington Post,* March 25, 2007, at: http://www.washingtonpost.com/wp-dyn/content/article/2007/03/24/AR2007032401152.html.

52   NewZeal, "Obama Was a New Party Member: Documentary Evidence," Oct. 23, 2008 at: http://newzeal.blogspot.com/2008/10/obama-file-41-obama-was-new-party.html.

53   Ibid.

54   Sara Karp, "Pushing Progressive Issues With a Focus on Faith," Religion News Service, http://www.beliefnet.com/Faiths/Christianity/Protestant/2005/03/Pushing-Progressive-Issues-With-A-Focus-On-Faith.aspx.

55   Originally on Fox News Channel. Undated. Can be viewed at: http://www.youtube.com/watch?v=VUbUBTlmAiA

56   Anthony B. Bradley, "The Marxist Roots of Black Liberation Theology," Acton Institute, April 2, 2008, at: http://www.acton.org/commentary/443_marxist_roots_of_black_liberation_theology.php.

57   Brian Ross and Rehab El-Buri, "Obama's Pastor: God Damn America, U.S. to Blame for 9/11," ABCNews, March 13, 2008, at: http://abcnews.go.com/Blotter/DemocraticDebate/story?id=4443788&page=1.

58   "Obama Pastor's Sermon: 'God Damn America,'" Fox News, March 14, 2008, at: http://www.foxnews.com/politics/elections/2008/03/14/obamas-spiritual-adviser-questioned-us-role-in-spread-of-hiv-sept-11-attacks/.

59   "Jeremiah Wright: The Full G-Damn America Sermon," YouTube.com, start at 1:54 at http://www.youtube.com/watch?v=9yqO55NAsrQ&NR=1.

60   Full transcript available at: http://www.foxnews.com/politics/elections/2008/04/28/transcript-rev-wright-at-the-national-press-club/.

61   Cliff Kincaid, "Controversial New Video of Obama's Pastor," Accuracy in Media, Nov. 1, 2009, at: http://www.aim.org/aim-column/controversial-new-video-of-obamas-pastor/.

62   "New Video: Rev. Wright Praises Magazine's 'No Nonsense Marxism,'" Breitbart.tv at: http://www.breitbart.tv/new-video-rev-wright-praises-magazines-no-nonsense-marxism/.

63   "People," United States of America, Factbook, Central Intelligence Agency, at: https://www.cia.gov/library/publications/the-world-factbook/geos/us.html#People.

64   Bob Unruh, "Obama Bows to Saudi King," WorldNetDaily.com, April 2, 2009, at: http://www.wnd.com/index.php?fa=PAGE.view&pageId=93696. May be viewed at YouTube at: http://www.

youtube.com/watch?v=9WIqW6UCeaY.

65   Barack Obama speech at Call to Renewal Conference, June 28, 2006, full transcript at: http://www.barackobama.com/2006/06/28/call_to_renewal_keynote_address.php and YouTube at 1:08 at: http://www.youtube.com/watch?v=35sGJrWKcmY&feature=related.

66   "Barack Obama on Faith," at http://www.barackobama.com/pdf/ObamaonFaith.pdf.

67   Compassion Forum transcript, CNN, April 12, 2008, at: http://transcripts.cnn.com/TRANSCRIPTS/0804/13/se.01.html.

68   Barack Obama, in Turkey, April 10, 2009, press conference, on YouTube at: http://www.youtube.com/watch?v=aMOiZB6KNko&NR=1.

69   Robert Knight, "Clueless in Obama Nation," Culture and Media Institute, Media Research Center, March 3, 2008, at: http://www.cultureandmediainstitute.org/articles/2008/20080303200132.aspx.

70   Call to Renewal address, op cit.

71   Barack Obama, "A Politics of Conscience," United Church of Christ, June 23, 2007, at: http://www.ucc.org/news/significant-speeches/a-politics-of-conscience.html.

72   Laurie Goodstein, "Openly Gay Episcopal Bishop to Deliver Invocation at Lincoln Memorial," The New York Times, Jan. 12, 2008, at: http://thecaucus.blogs.nytimes.com/2009/01/12/openly-gay-episcopal-bishop-to-deliver-invocation-at-lincoln-memorial/.

73   Ed Whelan, "Seventh Circuit Nominee David Hamilton: 'Allah' Yes; 'Jesus' No," National Review Online at: http://bench.nationalreview.com/post/?q=ZmRiZGVkYzZmZGFhMDM4MTE2ZmE1ZTMxOTAxM2RkNmM=.

74   Fred Lucas, "Obama Names Pope-Basher to Faith-Based Initiative Board," CNSNews.com, April 6, 2009, at: http://www.cnsnews.com/Public/content/article.aspx?RsrcID=46192.

75   Julia Duin, "Obama at Georgetown: The mystery of the missing sign," The Washington Times, April 15, 2009, at: http://www.washingtontimes.com/weblogs/belief-blog/2009/apr/15/obama-at-georgetown-the-mystery-of-the-missing-sig/.

76   "Americans United Commends Obama for Discontinuing Religious Right-Focused Prayer Event at White House," Americans United for the Separation of Church and State, press release, May 5, 2009, at: http://members.au.org/site/News2?abbr=pr&page=NewsArticle&id=10425.

77   Ann Sanner, "Obama Hosts Dinner for Islamic Holy Month," Associated Press, Sept. 1, 2009, at: http://abcnews.go.com/Politics/wireStory?id=8466477.

78   Obama's Notre Dame Commencement Speech," transcript, May 17, 2009, The New York Times, at: http://www.nytimes.com/2009/05/17/us/politics/17text-obama.html.

79   Adapted and expanded from Robert Knight, "Obama Nation's Low View of Christianity," Townhall.com, June 8, 2009, at: http://townhall.com/columnists/RobertKnight/2009/06/08/obama_nations_low_view_of_christianity.

80   "Barack Obama on Abortion," On the Issues, at: http://www.ontheissues.org/Social/Barack_Obama_Abortion.htm.

81   SB 1095 summary, 92nd General Assembly, Illinois, at: http://www.ilga.gov/legislation/legisnet92/summary/920SB1095.html, and "Obama and 'Infanticide,'" FactCheck.org, Annenberg Public Policy Center, Aug. 25, 2008, at: http://www.factcheck.org/elections-2008/obama_and_infanticide.html.

82   Illinois Senate transcript, April 4, 2002, http://ilga.gov/senate/transcripts/strans92/ST040402.pdf, pp. 29-33.

83   Douglas Johnson, "Obama Cover-up on Born Alive Abortion Survivors Continues to Unravel After Sen. Obama Says NRLC Is 'Lying,'" National Right to Life, August 18, 2008, at: http://www.nrlc.org/ObamaBaipa/Obamacoveruponbornalive.htm.

84   "The Truth Behind False, Outrageous Lies about Obama and 'Born Alive' Legislation,"

Organizing for America Website at: http://factcheck.barackobama.com/
factcheck/2008/08/19/fact_check_born_alive_1.php.

85   Johnson, NRLC, op cit.

86   Jill Stanek's blog, Feb. 19, 2008, at: http://www.jillstanek.com/archives/2008/02/links_to_
barack.html.

87   United States Senate Roll Call Votes, 2009, at: http://www.senate.gov/legislative/LIS/
roll_call_lists/roll_call_vote_cfm.cfm?congress=109&session=2&vote=00216.

88   See co-sponsor list for S.1173, at http://thomas.loc.gov/cgi-bin/bdquery/
z?d110:SN01173:@@@P.

89   "Reproductive health care will be 'at the heart' of health care reform," Politifact, *St.
Petersburg Times*, at: http://www.politifact.com/truth-o-meter/promises/promise/519/
reproductive-health-care-will-be-heart-health-care/.

90   "Obama on Abortion: A Summary," MoralAccountability.com, at http://www.
moralaccountability.com/obama-on-abortion.

91   L. David Alinsky, "Saul Alinsky's son: 'Obama learned his lesson well,'" at: http://www.boston.com/
bostonglobe/editorial_opinion/letters/articles/2008/08/31/son_sees_fathers_handiwork_in_
convention/?s_campaign=8315.

92   Saul D. Alinsky, *Rules for Radicals: A Pragmatic Primer for Realistic Radicals* (New York: Vintage
Books, a division of Random House, 1989, originally published by Random House in 1971).

93   Ibid., dedication page.

94   Sol Stern, "Acorn's Nutty Regime for Cities," *City Journal*, Manhattan Institute, Spring 2003, at:
http://www.city-journal.org/html/13_2_acorns_nutty_regime.html.

95   John Fund, "A Victory Against Voter Fraud," *The Wall Street Journal*, April 29, 2008, at: http://
online.wsj.com/article/SB120943129695651437.html?mod=opinion_main_commentaries.

96   Ibid.

97   Stern, op cit.

98   Richard Andrew Cloward and Frances Fox Piven, "The Weight of the Poor: A Strategy to End
Poverty," *The Nation*, May 2, 1966, at: http://www.discoverthenetworks.org/Articles/A%20
Strategy%20to%20End%20Poverty2.html.

99   "The Cloward-Piven Strategy," Discoverthenetworks.org at: http://www.discoverthenetworks.org/
groupProfile.asp?grpid=6967.

100   Quoted in "The Cloward-Piven Strategy," op cit.

101   Robert B. Carleson, *Government Is the Problem: Memoirs of Ronald Reagan's Welfare
Reformer* (Alexandria, Va.: American Civil Rights Union, 2009), p. 139.

102   Robert Rector and Katherine Bradley, "Stimulus Bill Abolishes Welfare Reform and Adds New
Welfare Spending," Heritage Foundation, Feb. 11, 2009, at: http://www.heritage.org/Research/
Welfare/wm2287.cfm.

103   United Press International, "U.S. debt ceiling raised," Dec. 17, 2009, at: http://www.upi.com/
Daily-Briefing/2009/12/17/US-debt-ceiling-raised/UPI-19821261058769/.

104   Eric Naing, "Senate Votes to Raise Federal Debt Limit," Open Congress, Jan. 28, 2010, at: http://
www.opencongress.org/articles/view/1499-Senate-Votes-To-Raise-Federal-Debt-Limit.

105   Quoted in Jeff Zeleny and Jackie Calmes, "Obama, Assembling Team, Turns to the Economy," *The
New York Times*, Nov. 6, 2008, at: http://www.nytimes.com/2008/11/07/us/politics/07obama.
html?_r=1&hp=&pagewanted=all.

106   Tim Graham, "Rahm Emanuel: 'Center to Center-Right?'" Newsbusters.org, Media Research
Center, Nov. 6, 2008, at: http://newsbusters.org/people/rahm-emanuel?page=2 (scroll down).

107   "Rahm Emanuel on Abortion," On the Issues.org, at: http://www.ontheissues.org/IL/Rahm_
Emanuel_Abortion.htm.

108 Rahm Emanuel on Civil Rights, On the Issues.org, at: http://www.ontheissues.org/Cabinet/ Rahm_Emanuel_Civil_Rights.htm

109 Ibid, at http://www.ontheissues.org/Cabinet/Rahm_Emanuel_Civil_Rights.htm

110 Suzanne Smalley, Evan Thomas, "Come, Oh Come Emanuel," Newsweek, April 14, 2008, at: http://www.newsweek.com/id/130605.

111 Quoted in Smalley, Thomas.

112 Joshua Green, "The Enforcer," Rolling Stone, Oct. 20, 2005, at: http://www.rollingstone.com/politics/story/8091986/the_enforcer.

113 Smalley, Thomas, op. cit.

114 Elisabeth Bumiller, "The Brothers Emanuel," The New York Times Magazine, June 15, 1997, at: http://www.nytimes.com/1997/06/15/magazine/the-brothers-emanuel.html.

115 Smalley, Thomas, op. cit.

116 Con Coughlin American Ally: Tony Blair and the War on Terror (New York: HarperCollins, 2006).

117 Green, Rolling Stone, op. cit.

118 Trevor Loudon, "The Anthony 'Van' Jones Scandal: Who is Behind the Appointment of a Communist as Green Jobs Czar in the Obama Administration?" reprinted at America's Survival, Inc., at: http://www.usasurvival.org/docs/LoudonrprtJones.pdf.

119 Cliff Kincaid, "The blogger who nailed Van Jones," Accuracy in Media, Sept. 7, 2009, at: http://www.aim.org/aim-column/the-blogger-who-nailed-van-jones/.

120 Scott Wilson, Juliet Eilperin, "In Adviser's Resignation, Vetting Bites Obama Again," The Washington Post, Sept. 7, 2009, at: http://www.washingtonpost.com/wp-dyn/content/article/2009/09/06/AR2009090601054.html.

121 Jarrett's comment can be viewed on YouTube at: http://www.youtube.com/watch?v=Ud_yNFnfrSI.

122 "Obama and the Left," Wall Street Journal, Sept. 8, 2009, at: http://online.wsj.com/article/SB10001424052970203440104574399452969175732.html.

123 Jonathan Weisman and Ben Casselman, "School Speech Released in Bid to Quell Controversy," Wall Street Journal, Sept. 8, 2009, at: http://online.wsj.com/article/SB125234166475590463.html.

124 Eliza Strickland, "The New Face of Environmentalism," East Bay Express, Nov. 2, 2005, at: http://www.truthout.org/article/eliza-strickland-the-new-face-environmentalism, and quoted in Loudon, op cit.

125 STORM, Reclaiming Revolution: History & lessons from the work of Standing Together to Organize a Movement, Spring, 2004, at: http://webpages.charter.net/westerfunk/STORMSummation.pdf.

126 David Westerfield, "Reclaiming Revolution: A History and Summation of STORM," Sept. 3, 2009, at: http://www.davidwesterfield.net/2009/09/reclaiming-revolution-history-and-summation-of-storm/.

127 Cliff Kincaid, "Damaging Disclosures in Van Jones Scandal," Accuracy in Media, Oct. 21, 2009, at: http://www.aim.org/aim-column/damaging-disclosures-in-van-jones-scandal/.

128 "People of Color Groups Gather to Stand In Solidarity With Arab Americans and to Mourn the East Coast Dead" rally announcement, Sept. 12, 2001, at: http://base21.jinbo.net/new/show/show.php?p_cd=0&p_dv=0&p_docnbr=17775.

129 Scott Johnson, "Van Jones's First Take on 9/11," Powerline blog, Sept. 5, 2009, at: http://www.powerlineblog.com/archives/2009/09/024446.php.

130 Chip Johnson, "Timing of Protest Is Suspect: Mumia supporters disrupt youth event," San Francisco Chronicle, Oct. 9, 1999, at: http://www.sfgate.com/cgi-bin/article.cgi?f=/c/a/1999/10/09/MN91787.DTL.

131 "Call for Oct. 22, 2006: Eleventh Annual National Day of Protest to Stop Police Brutality,

Repression, and the Criminalization of a Generation," at: http://www.rwor.org/a/066/022-en. html. Jones signed it as a representative of the Ella Baker Center for Human Rights, a group he founded in 1996 and which describes itself as "a strategy and action center working for justice, opportunity and peace in urban America."

132   Amanda Carpenter, "Another apology may be coming from Van Jones," *The Washington Times*, Sept. 4, 2009, at: http://www.washingtontimes.com/weblogs/back-story/2009/sep/04/another-apology-may-be-coming-from-van-jones/.

133   Peter Ferrara, "All the President's Nuts," *American Spectator*, Sept. 9, 2009, at: http://spectator.org/archives/2009/09/09/all-the-presidents-nuts.

134   Press release on FCC appointees, July 29, 2009, Federal Communications Commission, at: http://hraunfoss.fcc.gov/edocs_public/attachmatch/DOC-292368A1.pdf.

135   FCC letter, Nov. 12, 2009, at: http://www.judicialwatch.org/files/documents/2009/fcc-marklloyd-docs-11122009.pdf.

136   Seton Motley, "Video: 'Diversity Czar' on Chavez's Venezuela: 'Incredible ... Democratic Revolution," Newsbusters.org, Media Research Center, August 28, 2009, at: http://newsbusters.org/blogs/seton-motley/2009/08/28/video-fcc-diversity-czar-chavezs-venezuela-incredible-democratic-revol.

137   Media Research Center, Aug. 26, 2009, at http://newsbusters.org/blogs/seton-motley/2009/08/28/video-fcc-diversity-czar-chavezs-venezuela-incredible-democratic-revol.

138   Motley, op. cit.

139   Ibid.

140   *The Structural Imbalance of Political Talk Radio*, a joint project of the Center for American Progress and the Free Press, June 21 and 22, 2007, at: http://www.americanprogress.org/issues/2007/06/pdf/talk_radio.pdf.

141   Cliff Kincaid, "Controversial New Video of Obama's Pastor," Accuracy in Media, Nov. 1, 2009, at: http://www.aim.org/aim-column/controversial-new-video-of-obamas-pastor/.

142   Ibid.

143   Ibid.

144   Matt Cover, "FCC's Diversity Officer Wants Private Broadcasters to Pay a Sum Equal to Their Total Operating Costs to Fund Public Broadcasting," CNSNews.com, August 12, 2009, at: http://www.cnsnews.com/news/article/52435, and *Structural Imbalance*, op. cit, p. 2.

145   Brian Fitzpatrick, *Unmasking the Myths Behind the Fairness Doctrine*, Culture and Media Institute, Media Research Center, 2008, p. 5 at: http://www.cultureandmedia.com/specialreports/2008/Fairness_Doctrine/CMI_FairnessDoctrine_Single.pdf

146   Ibid, p.10.

147   Robert H. Knight, *Not Fair, Not Free: The Fairness Doctrine Campaign to Crush Free Speech* (Fort Lauderdale, Fla.: Coral Ridge Ministries, 2009), p. 8.

148   Duties and Responsibilities of Associate General Counsel and Chief Diversity Officer, FCC, at: http://www.judicialwatch.org/files/documents/2009/fcc-marklloyd-docs-11122009.pdf.

149   Quoted in Bob Unruh, "Americans Alarmed at Attacks on Free Speech," WorldNetDaily.com, Oct. 27, 2009, at: http://www.wnd.comr/index.php?pageId=114195.

150   "Department of Safe and Drug Free Schools," AllGov.com, at: http://www.allgov.com/Agency/Office_of_Safe_and_Drug_Free_Schools.

151   Linda Harvey, "Children at Risk: GLSEN, Corruption and Crime," Mission America at: http://www.missionamerica.com.

152   "Obama's Buggery Czar," *The Washington Times*, Dec. 8, 2009, p. A-20, at: http://www.washingtontimes.com/news/2009/dec/08/obamas-buggery-czar/.

153   Jim Hoft, "Breaking: Obama's "Safe Schools Czar" Is Promoting Child Porn in the Classroom

— Kevin Jennings and the GLSEN Reading List," GatewayPundit.com, Dec. 4, 2009, at http://gatewaypundit.firstthings.com/2009/12/breaking-obamas-safe-schools-czar-is-promoting-porn-in-the-classroom-kevin-jennings-and-the-glsen-reading-list/.

154   "The 'Fistgate' incident: What homosexual activists in schools do to children," Massresistance.com at http://massresistance.com/docs/issues/fistgate/index.html. Warning: graphic language.

155   "'Safe Schools' czar Kevin Jennings helps Harvard celebrate homosexual terrorist group 'Act Up,'" Massresistance.com, Oct, 21, 2009, at: http://massresistance.com/docs/gen/09d/harvard_actup/index.html. Warning: graphic language and graphic images.

156   Brian Burt, "GLSEN's Jennings: 'That Is Our Mission from this Day Forward,'" *Lambda Report on Homosexuality*, January/February 1998, p. 5, cited in Peter LaBarbera, "When Silence Would Have Been Golden," Concerned Women for America, 2002, at http://www.cultureandfamily.org/articledisplay.asp?id=2580&department=CFI&categoryid=papers#ref.

157   "Harry Hay on Man/Boy Love," North American Man/Boy Love Association website, 2003, at Americans for Truth website, http://www.nambla.org/hayonmanboylove.htm.

158   LaBarbera, op. cit.

159   "At the President's Pleasure," editorial, *The Washington Times*, Sept. 28, 2009, at: http://www.washingtontimes.com/news/2009/sep/28/at-the-presidents-pleasure/.

160   Linda Harvey, "Bill Ayers' 'gay' agenda for your kids," WorldNetDaily, Oct. 13, 2008, at: http://www.wnd.com/index.php?pageId=77640.

161   "Cruising gay bars with the 'safe schools czar,'" editorial, *The Washington Times*, Dec. 11, 2009, p. A-20, at: http://washingtontimes.com/news/2009/dec/11/cruising-gay-bars-with-the-safe-schools-39727871/.

162   "After one year of gay "marriage" in Massachusetts," Massresistance.com, 2005. Description of the booklet has a link to the actual booklet. Warning. The article about the booklet is well edited, but the booklet itself contains extremely graphic imagery and language. Article is here: http://www.article8.org/docs/news_events/glsen_043005/conference.htm.

163   *Little Black Book: V 2.0 Queer in the 21st Century*, AIDS Action Committee, Boston, with assistance from the Massachusetts Department of Public Health, et al, 2005.

164   "Remarks of the President-Elect Barack Obama Science Team Roll-Out Radio Address," Friday, Dec. 17, 2008, Change.gov, the Office of the President-Elect, at: http://change.gov/newsroom/entry/the_search_for_knowledge_truth_and_a_greater_understanding_of_the_world_aro.

165   Angie Drobnic Holan, "Obama Appoints Holdren as Science Advisor," *St. Petersburg Times* Politifact, May 13, 2009, at: http://www.politifact.com/truth-o-meter/promises/promise/346/appoint-an-assistant-to-the-president-for-science-/.

166   Paul Ehrlich, Anne Ehrlich, and John Holdren. *Ecoscience: Population, Resources, and Environment* (San Francisco: W. H. Freeman and Company, 1977).

167   Ben Johnson, "Obama's Biggest Radical," Frontpagemag.com, Feb. 27, 2009, at: http://97.74.65.51/readArticle.aspx?ARTID=34198.

168   Cited in Joseph Abrams, "Obama's Science Czar Considered Forced Abortions, Sterilization as Population Growth Solutions," FoxNews.com, July 21, 2009, at: http://www.foxnews.com/politics/2009/07/21/obamas-science-czar-considered-forced-abortions-sterilization-population-growth/.

169   John P. Holdren, "Convincing the skeptics," *The New York Times*, Aug. 4, 2008, at: http://www.nytimes.com/2008/08/04/opinion/04iht-edholdren.1.14991915.html.

170   John P. Holdren, Presidential Address: Science and Technology for Sustainable Well-Being," adapted from the Presidential Address he delivered at the American Association for the Advancement of Science at the AAS Annual Meeting in San Francisco on February 15, 2007, and reported in *Science* 25, January 2008, Vol. 319, no. 5862, pp. 424-434, at: http://www.

sciencemag.org/cgi/content/full/319/5862/424.

171   Ibid.

172   R. Warren Anderson and Dan Gainor, "Fire and Ice: Journalists have warned of climate change for 100 years, but can't decide whether we face an ice age or warming," Special Report, Business and Media Institute, Media Research Center, 2007, at: http://www.businessandmedia. org/specialreports/2006/fireandice/fireandice.asp.

173   Ibid.

174   Ibid.

175   Ibid.

176   Jerome Corsi, "Science czar's guru called for more carbon: CO_2 promoted as greenhouse gas needed to fight global starvation," WorldNetDaily, Dec. 7, 2009, at: http://www.wnd.com/index. php?fa=PAGE.view&pageId=118304.

177   Ibid.

178   Ibid.

179   As quoted in Michelle Malkin, "Ghoulish Science Plus Obamacare Equals Health Hazard," July 24, 2009, in Townhall at: http://townhall.com/columnists/MichelleMalkin/2009/07/24/ghoulish_ science_plus_obamacare_equals_health_hazard, and cited in Wheeler and Leitner in *Shadow Government*, op cit., p. 165.

180   Quoted in Wheeler and Leitner, *Shadow Government*, p. 164.

181   Malkin, in "Ghoulish Science," op. cit.

182   See Robert H. Knight, *Fighting for America's Soul* (Fort Lauderdale, Fla.: Coral Ridge Ministries, 2009), p. 19.

183   Dr. Tim Ball and Judi McLeod, "Obama's Science Czar John Holdren Involved in Unwinding 'Climategate' Scandal," Canada Free Press, Nov. 24, 2009, at: http://www.canadafreepress.com/ index.php/article/17183.

184   Intergovernmental Panel on Climate Change website at: http://www.ipcc.ch/7g0_nobel_ popup.htm.

185   Terry Hurlbut, "John Holdren also involved in CRU e-mails," Nov. 24, 2009, at examiner.com at: http://www.examiner.com/x-28973-Essex-County-Conservative-Examiner~y2009m11d24-John-Holdren-also-involved-in-CRU-emails.

186   Global Warming Petition, with article by Arthur B. Robinson, Noah E. Robinson, and Willie Soon, "Environmental Effects of Increased Atmospheric Carbon Dioxide," Oregon Institute of Science and Medicine, *Journal of American Physicians and Surgeons* (2007) 12, 79-90, at http://www. petitionproject.org.

187   From *An Essay on the Principle of Population: Or a View of Its Past and Present Effects on Human Happiness; with an Inquiry Into Our Prospects Respecting the Future Removal or Mitigation of the Evils which It Occasions*, (1798) Book IV, Chapter V, *Of the Consequences of pursuing the opposite Mode, IV.V.1*, Library of Economics and Liberty at: http://www.econlib. org/library/Malthus/malPlong30.html

188   "Carol Browner Joins Board of APX," press release, March 10, 2008, at: http://www.apx.com/ news/pr-Carol-Browner-Joins-APX-Board.asp.

189   http://www.americanprogress.org/.

190   Obama Climate Czarina Was a Member of Socialist Group's Environmental Commission, FoxNews. com, January 15, 2009, at: http://www.foxnews.com/story/0,2933,479935,00.html.

191   "About Us," Socialist International website at: http://www.socialistinternational.org/about.cfm

192   See http://www.socialistinternational.org/viewArticle.cfm?ArticlePageID=1272.

193   "Browner is an environmental radical — and a socialist (seriously)." Editorial, *The Washington Examiner*, January 8, 2009, at: http://www.washingtonexaminer.com/opinion/Browner_is_an_

environmental_radical_and_a_socialist_seriously_010809.html.

194   FoxNews.com, "Obama Climate Czarina Was Member of Socialist Group's Environmental Commission," Jan. 15, 2009, at: http://www.foxnews.com/story/0,2933,479935,00.html.

195   Quoted in David A. Patten, "All the President's Czars," *Newsmax* magazine, December 2009, p. 60.

196   FoxNews.com, op. cit.

197   Mark Tapscott, "'Put nothing in writing,' Browner told auto execs on secret White House CAFE talks; Sensenbrenner wants investigation," *Washington Examiner*, July 8, 2009, at: http://www.washingtonexaminer.com/opinion/blogs/beltway-confidential/Put-nothing-in-writing-Browner-told-auto-execs-on-secret-White-House-CAFE-talks-50260677.html.

198   "FNC's Steve Doocy Presses Carol Browner on Cap-and-Trade Bill," Newsbusters.org, Media Research Center, at http://newsbusters.org/blogs/nb-staff/2009/06/29/fncs-steve-doocy-presses-carol-browner-cap-trade-bill and cited in Scott Wheeler, Peter Leitner, *Shadow Government: What Obama Doesn't Want You to Know About His Czars* (Washington, D.C.: National Republican Trust PAC, 2009), p. 83.

199   International Panel on Climate Change website at http://www.ipcc.ch/organization/organization.htm.

200   Stephen Dinan, "Climate 'czar' says hacked e-mails don't change anything," *The Washington Times*, Nov. 25, 2009, at: http://www.washingtontimes.com/news/2009/nov/25/climate-czar-says-e-mails-dont-change-anything/.

201   Cass R. Sunstein and Martha C. Nussbaum, *Animal Rights: Current Debates and New Directions* (Oxford University Press, USA), 2004, cited in Wheeler and Leitner, op. cit., p. 143.

202   Sunstein and Nussbaum, *Animal Rights*, pp. 259-260, quoted at "Sunstein Quotes" at: http://stopsunstein.com/media/pdf/Sunstein%20quote%20file.pdf.

203   Wheeler and Leitner, op. cit., p. 144.

204   April 24, 2007. Entire conference can be viewed at: http://video.google.com/videoplay?doc id=2586700172704318361# or accessed through the McCarville Report Online at: http://wwwtmrcom.blogspot.com/2009/03/opinion-most-dangerous-man-in-america.html.

205   Ibid, at 49:29.

206   Ibid, at 50:15 to 51.

207   Ibid.

208   Quoted in Aaron Klein, "Sunstein urges: Abolish marriage," WorldNetDaily.com, Oct. 23, 2009, at: http://www.wnd.com/index.php?pageId=113802.

209   Ibid.

210   Quoted in Aaron Klein, "Sunstein: Take organs from 'helpless patients,'" WorldNetDaily.com, Oct. 12, 2009, at: http://www.wnd.com/index.php?pageId=112757.

211   Ibid.

212   Aaron Klein, "Sunstein: Government must fund abortion," WorldNetDaily.com, Sept. 29, 2009, at: http://www.wnd.com/index.php?pageId=111370.

213   Cass R. Sunstein, *Democracy and the Problem of Free Speech* (New York: The Free Press,1995) p. 92, as cited in "Sunstein Quotes," at: http://stopsunstein.com/media/pdf/Sunstein%20quote%20file.pdf.

214   Cass R. Sunstein, Republic.com 2.0 (Princeton, New Jersey: Princeton University Press, 2007), p. 137. A PDF version of the page can be read on the Web at: http://stopsunstein.com/media/pdf/Quote%206%20-%20A%20system%20of%20limitless%20individual....pdf.

215   Bloggingheads.tv, Cass R. Sunstein, University of Chicago Law School and Eugene Volokh, The Volokh Conspiracy, UCLA Law School video debate, recorded May 27, 2008 and posted June 2, 2008, and cited at "Sunstein Quotes," op. cit.

216   Ibid.

217   Cited in Wheeler and Leitner, p. 145.

218   Ibid., quoting Cass Sunstein, *A Constitution of Many Minds* (Princeton, New Jersey: Princeton University Press, 2009), pp. 172-173.

219   Sunstein, *A Constitution of Many Minds* (Princeton, New Jersey: Princeton University Press, 2009), p. 5, quoted on "Cass Sunstein Quotes" at: http://stopsunstein.com/media/pdf/Sunstein%20quote%20file.pdf.

220   Ibid.

221   Ken Blackwell and Ken Klukowski, "Gun Case or Pandora's Box?" *The Washington Times*, Dec. 11, 2009, and the American Civil Rights Union at: http://www.theacru.org/acru/ken_blackwell_and_ken_klukowski_a_gun_case_or_pandoras_box/.

222   Cass R. Sunstein, *The Second Bill of Rights: FDR's Unfinished Revolution and Why We Need It More Than Ever* (New York: Basic Books, 2004), p. 1, as cited in Wheeler and Leitner, op. cit., pp. 145-146.

223   "The Pursuit of John Yoo," editorial, *The Wall Street Journal*, June 25, 2009, at: http://online.wsj.com/article/SB124580586602845075.html.

224   Ibid.

225   Harold Koh, "International Law as Part of Our Law," 98 *American Journal of International Law* 43, 48, 52 (2004), cited by M. Edward Whelan III, "Harold Koh's Transnationalism," *National Review Online's* Bench Memos, April 16, 2009, at: http://www.eppc.org/publications/pubID.3793/pub_detail.asp.

226   John Fonte, "Transnational Progressive Nominated as Legal Advisor for State," The Corner, *National Reivew Online*, March 24, 2009, at: http://corner.nationalreview.com/post/?q=MDBhMDk5NzFkZGIwMDIOZDM3ZDQzYzBjNTk1ODg0YmQ=.

227   *Amicus* brief in *Lawrence v. Texas*, http://supreme.lp.findlaw.com/supreme_court/briefs/02-102/02-102.mer.ami.ai.pdf, at p. 17.

228   Justice Antonin G. Scalia, dissenting in *Lawrence v. Texas*, at: http://www.law.cornell.edu/supct/html/02-102.ZD.html.

229   Harold Koh, testimony before the Senate Foreign Relations Committee, June 2002, cited by Whelan, op. cit.

230   M. Edward Whelan III, "Harold Koh's Transnationalism," *National Review Online's* Bench Memos, April 16, 2009, at: http://www.eppc.org/publications/pubID.3793/pub_detail.asp.

231   "Dr. Stephen Chu, Secretary of Energy," U.S. Department of Energy, bio at: http://www.energy.gov/organization/dr_steven_chu.htm.

232   Quoted in Ian Talley, "Steven Chu: Americans Are Like 'Teenage Kids' When It Comes to Energy," *The Wall Street Journal*, Sept. 21, 2009, WSJ blogs at: http://blogs.wsj.com/environmentalcapital/2009/09/21/steven-chu-americans-are-like-teenage-kids-when-it-comes-to-energy/.

233   "EPA Announces Fall Tour to Help Americans Fight Climate Change and Save Money," Sept. 17, 2009, Environmental Protection Agency press release at: http://yosemite.epa.gov/opa/admpress.nsf/0/fb4e2d1b681bbde08525763400535c12?OpenDocument.

234   Major Garret, "Energy Secretary Offers Dire Global Warning Prediction," FoxNews.com, April 19, 2009, at: http://www.foxnews.com/politics/2009/04/19/energy-secretary-offers-dire-global-warming-prediction/.

235   Louise Gray, "Obama's green guru calls for white roofs," *The Telegraph*, May 27, 2009, at: http://www.telegraph.co.uk/earth/earthnews/5389278/Obamas-green-guru-calls-for-white-roofs.html.

236   Neil King Jr. and Stephen Power, "Times Tough for Energy Overhaul," *The Wall Street Journal*,

Dec. 12, 2008, at: http://online.wsj.com/article/SB122904040307499791.html.

237   From the transcript of the hearing: REP. CLIFF STEARNS, R-Fla.: Last September you made a statement that somehow we have to figure out how to boost the price of gasoline to the levels in Europe, which at the time exceeded $8 a gallon. As Secretary of Energy, will you speak for or against any measures that would raise the price of gasoline?
SEC. CHU: As Secretary of Energy, I think especially now in today's economic climate, it would be completely unwise to want to increase the price of gasoline. And so we are looking forward to reducing the price of transportation in the American family. And this is done by encouraging fuel-efficient cars; this is done by developing alternative forms of fuel like biofuels that can lead to a separate source, an independent source of transportation fuel.
REP. STEARNS: But you can't honestly believe that you want the American people to pay for gasoline at the prices, the level in Europe?
SEC. CHU: No, we don't.
REP. STEARNS: No. But somehow, your statement, "Somehow we have to figure out how to boost the price of gasoline to the levels in Europe," doesn't that sound a little bit silly in retrospect for you to say that?
SEC. CHU: Yes.
"Press Release: House Energy & Commerce Committee, April 21-23," at http://republicans. energycommerce.house.gov/News/PRArticle.aspx?NewsID=6948.

238   Dr. William Gray, "Puncturing the Climate Balloon," Climatedepot.com, Dec. 8, 2009, at http://www.climatedepot.com/a/4369/Hurricane-Expert-Rips-Climate-Fears-There-has-been-an-unrelenting-quarter-century-of-onesided-indoctrination.

239   Robert Knight, "Obama's Porn King at Justice," The Washington Times, March 18, 2009, at: http://www.washingtontimes.com/news/2009/mar/18/obamas-porn-king-at-justice.

240   Knox v. United States, __ U.S. __, 114 S. Ct. 375 (1993), at: http://caselaw.lp.findlaw.com/cgi-bin/getcase.pl?court=3rd&navby=docket&no=940734p.

241   "President Obama Announces More Key Administration Posts," The White House, Sept. 14, 2009, at http://www.whitehouse.gov/the_press_office/President-Obama-Announces-More-Key-Administration-Posts-9/14/09/.

242   "Employment Non-Discrimination Act of 2009," at: http://www.govtrack.us/congress/bill.xpd?bill=h111-3017.

243   Author heard Miss Feldblum make this remark after an Ethics and Public Policy seminar on gay rights and religious freedom in Washington, D.C., in the late 1990s.

244   Chai R. Feldblum, "Moral Conflict and Liberty: Gay Rights and Religion," The Becket Fund, undated, at: http://www.becketfund.org/files/4bce5.pdf. An earlier version of this paper was presented at a symposium at Brooklyn Law School and is published at 72 BROOKLYN L. REV. 61 (2006). This paper was also delivered in an abbreviated draft form at a Becket Fund for Religious Liberty meeting in 2005.

245   Chai Feldblum speech, Nov. 15, 2004, which can be viewed at Beetle Blogger, Oct. 10, 2009, at: http://beetlebabee.wordpress.com/2009/10/10/obamas-chai-feldblum-gay-sex-is-morally-good-government-has-a-duty-to-promote/.

246   "The Matthew Shepard and James Byrd, Jr. Hate Crimes Prevention Act," was an amendment to the Department of Defense Appropriations bill for 2010 that was signed into law on Oct. 28, 2009. by President Obama: Public Law No. 111-84 (the full text of the bill was not available on government websites as of Dec. 11, 2009).

247   "Beyond Same-Sex Marriage: A New Strategic Vision For All Our Families & Relationships," July 26, 2006, at: http://www.beyondmarriage.org/BeyondMarriage.pdf.

248   "The simple case against Chai Feldblum," Oct. 22, 2009, at: http://www.

americanprinciplesproject.org/topics/statements/424-the-simple-case-against-chai-feldblum.
html.

249   Chai R. Feldblum, "Gay Is Good: The Moral Case For Marriage Equality And More," at: http://www.
law.georgetown.edu/moralvaluesproject/Library/Papers/Feldblum_Gay_is_Good_Marriage.pdf.

250   Ken Blackwell and Ken Klukowski, *The Blueprint: Obama's Plan to Subvert the Constitution and
Build an Imperial Presidency* (Guildford, Conn.: Lyons Press, 2010).

251   Ken Klukowski, *"What Kagan Nomination Tells Us About Obama,"* Townhall.com, May 10, 2010,
at: http://townhall.com/columnists/KenKlukowski/2010/05/10/what_kagan_nomination_tells_us_
about_obama.

252   Mark Alexander, "Komrad Kagan + More," *Patriot Post*, May 13, 2010, at papundits: http://
papundits.wordpress.com/2010/05/13/komrade-kagan-more/.

253   Klukowski, *"What Kagan Nomination Tells Us About Obama."*

254   Matt Kelley, "Possible Supreme Court pick had ties with Goldman-Sachs," *USA Today*, April 27,
2010, at: http://www.usatoday.com/news/washington/judicial/2010-04-26-kagan_N.htm.

255   Elena Kagan, "Private Speech, Public Purpose: The Role of Governmental Motive in First
Amendment Doctrine," *The University of Chicago Law Review*, Vol. 63, No. 2 (Spring, 1996), pp.
413-517.

256   Horace Cooper, "Kagan's Troubling Record on the First Amendment," FoxNews.com, June 2, 2010,
at: http://www.foxnews.com/opinion/2010/06/02/horace-cooper-elena-kagan-amendment/.

257   Elena Kagan, Solicitor General, Brief for the United States in *United States vs. Robert J. Stevens*,
June 2009, at: http://www.abanet.org/publiced/preview/briefs/pdfs/07-08/08-769_Petitioner.
pdf.

258   Horace Cooper, "Kagan's Troubling Record on the First Amendment," FoxNews.com, June 2, 2010,
at: http://www.foxnews.com/opinion/2010/06/02/horace-cooper-elena-kagan-amendment/.

259   Ibid.

260   *Citizens United v. Federal Election Commission*, No. 09-205, Jan. 21, 2010, at: http://www.law.
cornell.edu/supct/html/08-205.ZS.html.

261   Memorandum for the President, May 13, 1997, "Daschle and Feinstein Amendments," William
J. Clinton Presidential Library and Museum, at http://www.clintonlibrary.gov/Documents/
Kagan%20-%20Bruce%20Reed/Kagan%20-%20Bruce%20Reed%20-%20Subject%20File%20
Series/Box%2097%20Abortion%20Doc%203.pdf.

262   *Doe v. Bolton*, 410, U.S. 179 (1973), at: http://caselaw.lp.findlaw.com/scripts/getcase.
pl?court=us&vol=410&invol=179.

263   Steven Ertelt, "Elena Kagan Helped Keep Partial-Birth Abortion Legal Longer, Pro-Life Group
Says," May 12, 2010, Lifenews.com. http://www.lifenews.com/nat6327.html.

264   Bethany Stotts, "Elena Kagan's Campus Activism," *Accuracy in Academia*, May 25, 2010, at:
http://www.academia.org/elena-kagans-campus-activism/.

265   Legal brief, *Forum for Academic and Institutional Rights vs. Rumsfeld*, et al, United States Court
of Appeals for the Third Circuit, (2003) at: http://www.law.georgetown.edu/solomon/documents/
OMelvenyLawProfs.pdf.

266   Stott, "Elena Kagan's Campus Activism."

267   Remarks by Elena Kagan at Peter Gruber Foundation Justice Prize presentation in 2006, at:
http://www.senate.gov/fplayers/I2009/urlOfficeOpenPlayer.cfm?fn=9093039100519112912
at 3:06.

268   Aharon Barak, *The Judge in a Democracy*, (Princeton: Princeton University Press, 2006), p.
179, cited in "Elena Kagan Calls Judicial Activist Judge Her Judicial Hero, Proudest Association,"
Lifenews.com, June 3, 2010, at: http://www.lifenews.com/nat6391.html.

269   Aharon Barak, *The Judge in a Democracy*, p. 193, cited in Lifenews.com, op. cit.

270   Elena Kagan, "To the Final Conflict: Socialism in New York City, 1900-1933," Princeton University, at http://www.scribd.com/full/31371092?access_key=key-2gn32lluxbdxjgf10w3j.

271   Michael Gaynor, "Read Elena Kagan's Princeton senior thesis yourself," RenewAmerica.com, May 20, 2010, at: http://www.renewamerica.com/columns/gaynor/100520.

272   Upton Sinclair, letter to Norman Thomas, 1951, quoted at Snopes.com, at: http://www.snopes.com/politics/quotes/socialism.asp.

273   Eric Holder Biography, Bio Website, at: http://www.biography.com/articles/Eric-Holder-391612?part=1.

274   Ibid.

275   Robert Longley, "Eric Holder: Attorney General," About.com, a *Washington Post* company, at: http://usgovinfo.about.com/od/thepresidentandcabinet/a/eric_holder.htm.

276   Carrie Johnson, "Holder Confirmed as the First Black Attorney General," *The Washington Post*, Feb. 3, 2009, at: http://www.washingtonpost.com/wp-dyn/content/article/2009/02/02/AR2009020202581.html.

277   Pierre Thomas and Jason Ryan, "Stinging Remarks on Race from Attorney General," *ABC News*, Feb. 18, 2009, at: http://abcnews.go.com/TheLaw/Story?id=6905255&page=1.

278   Richard Cohen, "Pardon My Exception," *The Washington Post*, Dec. 2, 2008, at: http://www.washingtonpost.com/wp-dyn/content/article/2008/12/01/AR2008120102403.html.

279   Fox News clip, Nov. 4, 2008, can be viewed at YouTube at: http://www.youtube.com/watch?v=H4o_8HtEIRQ.

280   Letter of resignation, J. Christian Adams, May 14, 2010, at: http://www.scribd.com/doc/31574180/J-Christian-Adams-resignation-letter-051910, and cited by J. P. Friere, "DOJ Voting Rights attorney resigns over Black Panthers Stonewalling," *The Washington Examiner*, May 18, 2010, at: http://www.washingtonexaminer.com/opinion/blogs/beltway-confidential/doj-voting-rights-attorney-resigns-over-black-panthers-stonewalling-94202249.html.

281   Judicial Watch, "JW Sues DOJ for Documents Regarding Decision to Dismiss of Lawsuit against New Black Panther Party for Self-Defense," press release, May 25, 2010, at: http://www.judicialwatch.org/news/2010/may/jw-sues-doj-documents-regarding-decision-dismiss-lawsuit-against-new-black-panther-par.

282   "Special Protection for Black Panthers," editorial, *The Washington Times*, Jan. 15, 2010, at: http://www3.washingtontimes.com/news/2010/jan/15/special-protection-for-black-panthers/print/.

283   Statement of Eric H. Holder, Jr., Deputy Attorney General, before the Committee on the Judiciary, U.S. Senate, May 11, 1999, concerning hate crimes, at: http://korvas-sux.appspot.com/www.justice.gov/archive/dag/testimony/daghate051199.htm.

284   "Hate Crimes Bill Stymied in Judiciary Committee," NOW Legislative Update, National Organization for Women, June 7, 1999, at http://www.now.org/issues/legislat/06-07-99.html#hate.

285   Eric H. Holder, Jr., "Testimony at a hearing entitled THE MATTHEW SHEPARD HATE CRIMES PREVENTION ACT OF 2009" on June 25, 2009, Committee of the Judiciary, U.S. Senate, at: http://judiciary.senate.gov/pdf/06-25-09HolderTestimony.pdf.

286   The final name of the bill was "The Matthew Shepard and James Byrd, Jr. Hate Crimes Prevention Act of 2009, at: http://www.justice.gov/crt/crim/249fin.php. Jon Ward, "Obama signs hate crimes bill," *The Washington Times*, Oct. 29, 2009, at: http://www.washingtontimes.com/news/2009/oct/29/obama-signs-hate-crimes-bill-into-law/.

287   Ibid.

288   Josh Meyer and Tom Hamburger, "Eric Holder pushed for controversial clemency," *Los Angeles Times*, Jan. 9, 2009, at: http://articles.latimes.com/2009/jan/09/nation/na-holder9.

289   Ken Blackwell and Ken Klukowski, "Defund Holder's Manhattan Transfer," originally at
        BigGovernment.com, and at American Civil Rights Union, Dec. 1, 2009, at: http://www.theacru.
        org/acru/ken_blackwell_and_ken_klukowski_defund_holders_manhattan_transfer/.

290   "Graham Presses Holder on Reading Osama bin Laden Miranda Rights," RealClearPolitics, Nov.
        18, 2009, at: http://www.realclearpolitics.com/video/2009/11/18/graham_presses_holder_on_
        reading_osama_bin_laden_miranda_rights.html.

291   The Fox Nation, "Holder Refuses to Say 'Radical Islam,'" May 13, at: http://www.thefoxnation.com/
        attorney-general-eric-holder/2010/05/13/watch-holder-refuses-say-radical-islam?page=7.

292   Ken Blackwell, "Dhimmicrats on the March?" AmericanThinker.com, May 25, 2010, at: http://www.
        americanthinker.com/2010/05/dhimmicrats_on_the_march.html.

293   "Holder: Feds may sue over Arizona immigration law," CNN.com, May 9, 2010, at: http://www.cnn.
        com/2010/POLITICS/05/09/holder.arizona.immigration/index.html.

294   Jake Tapper, "President Obama Says Arizona's 'Poorly-Conceived' Immigration Law Could Mean
        Hispanic-Americans Are Harassed," ABCNews.com, April 27, 2010, at: http://blogs.abcnews.com/
        politicalpunch/2010/04/president-obama-says-arizonas-poorlyconceived-immigration-law-
        could-mean-hispanicamericans-are-haras.html.

295   Arizona House Bill 2162 (2010) at: http://www.tucsonsentinel.com/files/pdf/hb2162.pdf..

296   "Holder Admits Not Reading Arizona's Immigration Law Despite Criticizing It," FoxNews.com,
        May 14, 2010, at: http://www.foxnews.com/politics/2010/05/13/holder-admits-reading-
        arizonas-immigration-law-despite-slamming/.

297   Ed Whelan, "Sotomayor and PRLDEF's Extreme Abortion Record," National Review Online Bench
        Memo, July 7, 2009, at: http://bench.nationalreview.com/post/?q=YjM2YWYyYWJkM2M5YmQxZ
        GNkYmU4NWZjNjljNjBjOTk

298   Ibid.

299   Charlie Savage, "A Judge's View of Judging Is on the Record," The New York Times, May 14,
        2009, at: http://www.nytimes.com/2009/05/15/us/15judge.html.

300   Colleen Raezlius, "Media Reports Silent on Obama HHS Pick Kathleen Sebelius' Pro-Abortion
        Record," LifeNews.com, March 8, 2009, (originally from Newsbusters.org) at: http://www.
        lifenews.com/state3924.html.

301   David S. Hilzenrath, "Objecting to 'Gag Order' on Insurers, Republicans Threaten to Delay
        HHS Confirmations," The Washington Post, Sept. 25, 2009, at: http://voices.washingtonpost.
        com/44/2009/09/24/objecting_to_gag_order_on_insu.html.

302   Brent Baker, "ABC Notices Obama Administration's Effort to Suppress Criticism of ObamaCare,"
        Newsbusters.org, Sept. 23, 2009, at: http://newsbusters.org/blogs/brent-baker/2009/09/23/
        abc-notices-obama-administrations-effort-suppress-criticism-obamacare.

303   Ed Whelan, "Seventh Circuit Nominee David Hamilton: 'Allah' Yes; 'Jesus' No," National Review
        Online at: http://bench.nationalreview.com/post/?q=ZmRiZGVkYzZmZGFhMDM4MTE2ZmE1ZTMx
        OTAxM2RkNmM=.

304   "Vote No on David Hamilton," Susan B. Anthony List press release, Christian Newswire, Nov. 17,
        2009, at: http://www.christiannewswire.com/news/9894812194.html.

305   Carl Tobias, "Elevating Judge David Hamilton to the Seventh Circuit," Findlaw.com, at: http://writ.
        news.findlaw.com/commentary/20091117_tobias.html.

306   Ibid. It should be noted that this article by Carl Tobias rebuts some of the criticism and
        supports Hamilton's nomination.

307   Kate Phillips, "More Obama Cabinet Nominees Approved," The New York Times, Jan. 22, 2009, at:
        http://thecaucus.blogs.nytimes.com/2009/01/22/more-obama-cabinet-nominees-confirmed/.

308   Nancy Sutley, Wikipedia, at: http://en.wikipedia.org/wiki/Nancy_Sutley#cite_note-CB-0.

309   Suzanne Goldenberg, "Nancy Sutley: Obama to stake political prestige on passing U.S. climate

bill," *The Guardian*, June 2, 2009, at: http://www.guardian.co.uk/environment/2009/jun/02/obama-climate-change-bill.

310   "OPM Director John Berry lauds passage of Domestic Partnership Benefits and Obligations Act through House Committee on Oversight and Government Management," press release, Office of Personnel Management, Nov. 18, 2009, at: http://www.opm.gov/news/opm-director-john-berry-lauds-passage-of-domestic-partnership-benefits-and-obligations-act-through-house-committee-on-oversight-and-government-management,1495.aspx.

311   John Berry, Memorandum from Office of Personnel Management, "Implementation of the President's Memorandum Regarding Extension of Benefits to Same-Sex Domestic Partners of Federal Employees," June 2, 2010, at: http://www.chcoc.gov/transmittals/TransmittalDetails.aspx?TransmittalID=2982.

312   Public Law 104-199, 104th Congress, The Defense of Marriage Act, at: http://frwebgate.access.gpo.gov/cgi-bin/getdoc.cgi?dbname=104_cong_public_laws&docid=f:publ199.104.pdf.

313   OPM Director John Berry Lauds Signing of Presidential Memorandum on the Extension of Benefits to Same-Sex Domestic Partners of Federal Employees, press release, U.S. Office of Personnel Management, June 2, 2010, at: http://boston.bizjournals.com/prnewswire/press_releases/District_of_Columbia/2010/06/02/DC14869.

314   Jake Tapper, "Dawn Johnsen Withdraws Her Nomination," ABCNews.com, April 9, 2010 at: http://blogs.abcnews.com/politicalpunch/2010/04/dawn-johnsen-withdraws-her-nomination.html.

315   "Filibuster a radical," editorial, *The Washington Times*, April 22, 2009, p. A-20, at: http://washingtontimes.com/news/2009/apr/22/filibuster-a-radical/.

316   Ibid.

317   Steven Ertelt, "Pro-Abortion Obama Pick Dawn Johnsen Withdraws Name for Justice Department Slot," Lifenews.com, April 11, 2010, at: http://www.lifenews.com/nat6238.html.

318   Steven Ertelt, "Obama Makes Lawyer for Terri Schiavo's Husband Third-Ranking Justice Official," LifeNews, com, Jan. 6, 2009, at: http://www.lifenews.com/bio2685.html.

319   Ibid.

320   Jerry Seper, "Exclusive: No. 3 at Justice OK'd Panther reversal," *The Washington Times*, July 30, 2009, at: http://www.washingtontimes.com/news/2009/jul/30/no-3-at-justice-okd-panther-reversal/.

321   Ibid.

322   Barack Obama, speaking at Democratic Party fundraiser in Hollywood, May 27, 2009, at: http://www.youtube.com/watch?v=PIBzNrzx5sE.

323   Rep. Michele Bachman, speaking on June 9, 2009 at: http://www.youtube.com/watch?v=thR-lVuztIY.

324   Joseph Gerth, "GOP's Higdon Captures Senate Seat," *Louisville Courier Journal*, Dec. 8, 2009, at: http://www.courier-journal.com/article/20091208/NEWS01/912080358/GOP%5C-s-Higdon-captures-Senate-seat.

325   Daily Presidential Tracking Poll, Rasmussen Reports, March 31, 2010, at: http://www.rasmussenreports.com/public_content/politics/obama_administration/daily_presidential_tracking_poll.

326   Peter Jennings, ABC News radio commentary, Nov. 14, 1994, "ABC News Argues Voters Don't Really Want Contract With America," Media Watch, Media Research Center, February 1995, at: http://www.mrc.org/mediawatch/1995/watch19950201.asp.

327   Robert H. Knight, *Fighting for America's Soul* (Fort Lauderdale, Fla.: Coral Ridge Ministries, 2009).

328   Dr. Jerry Newcombe, *The Book That Made America* (Ventura, Calif.: Nordskog Publishing, Inc., 2009), p. 229.

329 M. Edward Whelan, "Harold Koh's Transnationalism—Treaties: CEDAW as a Case Study (Part 1)," *National Review Online*, April 13, 2009, at: http://bench.nationalreview.com/post/?q=MTQ1ZDAO ZDYwMDVkNjNiYTgwNDJhODU0YTI2NmQwNDk=.

330 "Concluding observations of the Committee on the Elimination of Discrimination Against Women: Mexico," May 14, 1998, A/53/38, paras. 354-427. At http://www.unhchr.ch/tbs/doc.nsf/ (Symbol)/f596e181b06a23cb80256664004f3c10?Opendocument.

331 "Concluding Observations of the Committee on the Elimination of Discrimination Against Women: Colombia," Feb. 5, 1999, A/54/38, paras. 337-401. At http://www.unhchr.ch/tbs/doc.nsf/ (Symbol)/0a318a243ffa4eff8025673200507f7a?Opendocument.

332 "Concluding Observations of the Committee on the Elimination of Discrimination Against Women: Italy," Aug. 12, 1997, A/52/38/Rev.1, Part II paras.322-364. At http://www.unhchr.ch/ tbs/doc.nsf/(Symbol)/39a6156c5dbe455380256500005a9aa0?Opendocument.

333 "Concluding Observations of the Committee on the Elimination of Discrimination Against Women: China," Feb. 5, 1999, A/54/38, paras. 251-336. At http://www.unhchr.ch/tbs/doc.nsf/(Sy mbol)/1483ffb5a2a626a980256732003e82c8?Opendocument.

334 "Concluding Observations of the Committee on the Elimination of Discrimination Against Women: Kyrgyzstan," Feb. 5, 1999, A/54/38, paras. 95-142. At http://www.unhchr.ch/tbs/doc. nsf/(Symbol)/b98a306cbf046296802567320051754a?Opendocument.

335 "Concluding Observations of the Committee on the Elimination of Discrimination Against Women: Ireland," June 25, 1999, A/54/38, paras.161-201. At http://www.unhchr.ch/tbs/doc.nsf/ (Symbol)/ad35ac0cac68033c802567f200543567?Opendocument.

336 "Concluding Observations of the Committee on the Elimination of Discrimination Against Women: Belarus," Feb. 4, 2000. A/55/38, paras. 334-378. At http://www.unhchr.ch/tbs/doc.nsf/ (Symbol)/84980f350885c64fc125695b00362673?Opendocument.

337 "Concluding Observations of the Committee on the Elimination of Discrimination Against Women: Austria," June 30, 2000, A/55/38, paras. 211-243. At http://www.unhchr.ch/tbs/doc. nsf/(Symbol)/ecb3113330b3e265c1256928005228cc?Opendocument.

338 "Concluding Observations of the Committee on the Elimination of Discrimination Against Women: Mexico," May 14, 1998, A/53/38, paras. 354-427. At http://www.unhchr.ch/tbs/doc.nsf/ (Symbol)/f596e181b06a23cb80256664004f3c10?Opendocument.

339 "Concluding Observations of the Committee on the Elimination of Discrimination Against Women: Denmark," Jan. 31, 1997, A/52/38/Rev.1, paras. 248-274. At http://www.unhchr.ch/tbs/ doc.nsf/(Symbol)/4e594c96a4ca6b3c8025649d002e7c5e?Opendocument.

340 "Concluding Observations of the Committee on the Elimination of Discrimination Against Women: Austria," June 30, 2000, A/55/38, paras. 211-243, At http://www.unhchr.ch/tbs/doc. nsf/(Symbol)/ecb3113330b3e265c1256928005228cc?Opendocument.

ACKNOWLEDGEMENTS

I would like to thank John Aman for his editing and good counsel about the direction of the book, Hector Padron, Jennifer Kennedy Cassidy and the leadership team at Truth in Action Ministries for continuing Dr. D. James Kennedy's legacy of informing the public from a Christian perspective, Susan Carleson for affording opportunities that helped make this book more compelling, and Greg Rohrbough for some timely and insightful research assistance.

APPENDIX

The United Nations' Convention on the Elimination of All Forms of Discrimination Against Women (CEDAW)

Here are some examples of the CEDAW committee's interpretations of the treaty's reach, as assembled by M. Edward Whelan III in his *National Review Online* Bench Memos. The opinions take a radical stance on "abortion, prostitution, lesbianism, religion, Mother's Day, 'gender studies,' 'redistribution of wealth,' comparable worth (not to be confused with equal pay), and quotas."[329] Whelan notes that Harold Koh, during a 2002 Senate hearing, either ducked these issues or seriously misrepresented them, while calling it a "national disgrace" that the Senate still had not ratified the treaty, which President Carter had signed in 1980.

ABORTION [MEXICO, MAY 14, 1998][330]

408. The Committee recommends that the Government consider the advisability of revising the legislation criminalizing abortion and suggests that it weigh the possibility of authorizing the use of the RU486 contraceptive, which is cheap and easy to use, as soon as it becomes available.

426. The Committee recommends that all states of Mexico should review their legislation so that, where necessary, women are granted access to rapid and easy abortion.

ABORTION [COLOMBIA, FEB. 5, 1999][331]

393. The Committee notes with great concern that abortion, which is the second cause of maternal deaths in Colombia, is punishable as an illegal act. No exceptions are made to that prohibition, including where the mother's life

is in danger or to safeguard her physical or mental health or in cases where the mother has been raped. The Committee is also concerned that women who seek treatment for induced abortions, women who seek an illegal abortion and the doctors who perform them are subject to prosecution. The Committee believes that legal provisions on abortion constitute a violation of the rights of women to health and life and of article 12 of the Convention.

ABORTION [ITALY, AUG. 12, 1997][332]

353. The Committee expressed particular concern with regard to the limited availability of abortion services for women in southern Italy, as a result of the high incidence of conscientious objection among doctors and hospital personnel.

PROSTITUTION [CHINA, FEB. 5, 1999][333]

288. The Committee is concerned that prostitution, which is often a result of poverty and economic deprivation, is illegal in China.

289. The Committee recommends decriminalization of prostitution.

LESBIANISM [KYRGYZSTAN, FEB. 5, 1999][334]

128. The Committee recommends that lesbianism be reconceptualized as a sexual orientation and that penalties for its practice be abolished.

RELIGION [IRELAND, JUNE 25, 1999][335]

180. The Committee notes that although Ireland is a secular State, the influence of the Church is strongly felt not only in attitudes and stereotypes but also in official State policy. In particular, women's right to health, including reproductive health, is compromised by this influence.

MOTHER'S DAY [BELARUS, FEB. 4, 2000][336]

361. The Committee is concerned by the continuing prevalence of sex-role stereotypes and by the reintroduction of such symbols as a Mothers' Day and a Mothers' Award, which it sees as encouraging women's traditional roles. It is also concerned whether the introduction of human rights and

gender education aimed at countering such stereotyping is being effectively implemented.

"GENDER STUDIES" [AUSTRIA, JUNE 30, 2000][337]

232. ...The Committee also calls upon the Government to introduce affirmative action to increase the appointment of women to academic posts at all levels and to integrate gender studies and feminist research in university curricula and research programmes.

"REDISTRIBUTION OF WEALTH" [MEXICO, MAY 14, 1998][338]

403. ...In view of the relatively high growth levels of the Mexican economy that have been mentioned, the Committee would welcome a more equitable redistribution of wealth among the population.

COMPARABLE WORTH [DENMARK, JAN. 31, 1997][339]

267. Temporary special measures should be maintained and strengthened, particularly in the areas of reducing unemployment among women; *ensuring that women and men receive equal pay for work of equal value*; increasing women's participation in private-sector decision-making; increasing the number of female university professors and researchers; and encouraging men to devote more time to child care and housework. Such initiatives should include quantitative targets, time limits for their achievement, specific measures and sufficient budgetary resources.

QUOTAS [AUSTRIA, JUNE 30, 2000][340]

238. The Committee is concerned at the decrease in women's representation in the legislature in the recent elections. The Committee recommends that the Government undertake in this respect temporary special measures, in accordance with article 4, paragraph 1, of the Convention, and consider, *inter alia*, the use of federal funding for political parties as an incentive for the increased representation of women in Parliament, as well as the application of quotas and numerical goals and measurable targets aimed at increasing women's political participation.

INDEX

ABOUT THE AUTHOR

ROBERT KNIGHT is Senior Writer and Washington, D.C., Correspondent for Truth in Action Ministries. The author of the new book, *Radical Rulers: The White House Elite Who Are Pushing America Toward Socialism*, he is a former news editor and writer for the *Los Angeles Times*. Mr. Knight directed the Media Research Center's Culture and Media Institute (2006-2008), the Culture & Family Institute at Concerned Women for America (2001-2006) and the Cultural Studies Program at the Family Research Council (1992-2001). He was a Media Fellow at the Hoover Institution at Stanford University (1989-1990).

A draftsman of the federal Defense of Marriage Act, Knight was instrumental in its passage in 1996. He is the author of *Fighting for America's Soul: How Sweeping Change Threatens Our Nation and What We Must Do* (Coral Ridge Ministries, 2009); *The Silencers: How Liberals Are Trying to Shut Down Media Freedom in the U.S.* (Coral Ridge Ministries, 2010) and *The Age of Consent: The Rise of Relativism and the Corruption of Popular Culture* (Spence Publishing, 1998, 2000).

Mr. Knight, who is also a Senior Fellow at the American Civil Rights Union, has appeared on all major TV news programs, including Fox News, CBS Evening News, the NBC Nightly News, ABC's World News Tonight, *Oprah*, *The O'Reilly Factor*, CNN, PBS, MSNBC, CNBC as well as National Public Radio, *Focus on the Family*, *Point of View*, *The G. Gordon Liddy Show*, *The Glenn Beck Show*, the BBC and American Family Radio. He has published articles in the *Los Angeles Times*, the *Washington Times*, *National Review*, *World* and the *Wall Street Journal* and writes regularly for Townhall.com, Human Events, WorldNetDaily, American Thinker and OneNewsNow.

Mr. Knight has Bachelor's and Master's degrees in political science from American University, lives in northern Virginia, attends a non-denominational Bible church and is married with children.